elementary

real life

acement tests

ort tests

nguage skills tests in
vo versions

eaking tests

riting tests

id year and end of year tests

ith Audio CD

TEST BOOK

with Audio CD

Make your mark!

DOMINIKA CHANDLER   MONIKA GALBARCZYK

T0385820

Pearson Education Limited
Edinburgh Gate
Harlow
Essex CM20 2JE
England
and Associated Companies throughout the world.

www.pearsonelt.com

First published 2010
Seventh impression 2019

ISBN: 978-1-4058-9719-8

Set in Myriad Pro 10.5/12.5pt
Printed by CPI Group (UK) Ltd, Croydon CR0 4YY

Acknowledgements

We are grateful to the following for permission to reproduce copyright material:

Extracts on pages 43 and 45 adapted from Battle of Hastings, this article is licensed under the terms of the GNU Free Documentation Licence, http://www.gnu.org/copyleft/fdl.html. It uses material from the Wikipedia article 'Battle of Hastings', http://en.wikipedia.org/wiki/Battle_of_Hastings; Extracts on pages 43 and 45 adapted from Battle of Hastings reenactment, this article is licensed under the terms of the GNU Free Documentation Licence, http://www.gnu.org/copyleft/fdl.html. It uses material from the Wikipedia article 'Battle of Hastings reenactment', http://en.wikipedia.org/wiki/Battle_of_Hastings_reenactment; Extract on page 59 adapted from How to be a couch potato, http://www.wikihow.com/Be-a-Couch-Potato, article provided by WikiHow, http://www.wikihow.com, a wiki building the world's largest, highest quality how-to manual. Please edit this article and find author credits at the original wikiHow article on 'How to be a couch potato'. Content on wikiHow can be shared under a Creative Commons Licence, http://creativecommons.org/ licenses/by-nc-sa/2.5/; Extract on page 59 adapted from Couch potato, this article is licensed under the terms of the GNU Free Documentation Licence, http://www.gnu.org/copyleft/fdl.html. It uses material from the Wikipedia article 'Couch potato', http://en.wikipedia.org/wiki/Couch_potato; Extract on pages 65-66 adapted from Leonardo da Vinci, this article is licensed under the terms of the GNU Free Documentation Licence, http://www.gnu.org/copyleft/fdl.html. It uses material from the Wikipedia article 'Leonardo da Vinci', http:// en.wikipedia.org/wiki/Leonardo_da_Vinci.

In some instances we have been unable to trace the owners of copyright material, and we would appreciate any information that would enable us to do so.

Photo acknowledgements

The publisher would like to thank the following for their kind permission to reproduce their photographs:

(Key: b-bottom; c-centre; l-left; r-right; t-top)

Alamy Images: Peter Horee 57bc; **Corbis:** Arthur Klonsky 57b; Kevin Dodge 57t; **Photolibrary.com:** Banana Stock 57tc

Every effort has been made to trace the copyright holders and we apologise in advance for any unintentional omissions. We would be pleased to insert the appropriate acknowledgement in any subsequent edition of this publication.

Cover image: Front: Photolibrary.com: Sammy Sammy/Mauritius

contents

introduction

Testing in *Real Life*

The tests in *Real Life* have three main objectives:

- to give students a clear indication of their progress and a sense of achievement;
- to provide teachers with information about their students' progress which in turn will help them make their teaching more effective;
- to prepare students for exams (in terms of language skills and test tasks).

Real Life offers a systematic approach to testing and evaluation:

- revision in the Students' Book (active study sections)
- Exam Trainer in the Workbook
- Self-assessment Tests and Exam Tests in the Workbook.

There are six Self-assessment Tests in the Workbook (one every two units). All these tests include a vocabulary and grammar component and a skills component (listening, reading and communication). The Self-assessment Tests prepare students for the Language and Skills Tests in the Test Book.

Test Book

The Test Book includes a variety of tests that can be used at different stages of the course.

Short Tests

There are 12 Short Tests, one for each unit. These are progress tests which revise and test the language material (grammar and vocabulary). The grammar tasks focus on the grammar points from the *Grammar2know* sections and the lexical tasks revise vocabulary from the *Words2know* sections in each unit.

The Short tests have a version A and B (both similar level of difficulty). Each test can be administered to two groups of students at the same time or one of the versions can be used at a later date, either for students who have missed the test or to check progress.

Language and Skills Tests

There are six Language and skills tests, which test language and skills after every two units. As well as grammar and vocabulary tasks, they include listening, reading and communication tasks. The task types in these tests reflect the examination tasks used for testing the above skills. The Language and skills tests have version A and B with a similar level of difficulty. They can be administered during one 45-minute lesson or divided into two shorter parts (Language, then Skills) and administered over two lessons. In the Skills part, students in groups A and B listen to the same recording and read the same text but answer different questions. The listening part should be administered first.

Roleplays

There are 12 roleplays in total – one for every unit in the Student's Book. The roleplays are designed to test students' knowledge of the speaking functions introduced in the Students' Book. We suggest students complete the task together with the teacher. For each roleplay, there is a list of prompts to help the conversation. It would be a good idea for the teacher to start each task. Students can do the task with a partner but as the second role is more difficult, the student should not be evaluated using the same assessment scales.

We suggest the following assessment criteria for the roleplays:

Assessment of the roleplays (10 marks)	
8–10 marks (very good)	– complete and clear communication of information suggested in the bullet points – varied grammatical and lexical structures (with minor but not frequent mistakes which do not affect communication) – fluent speech (with minor disturbances in the flow of speech) and correct and clear pronunciation (with minor mistakes)
5–7 marks (pass)	– mostly/partly clear communication of information suggested in the bullet points – sufficient grammatical and lexical structures (with minor, frequent mistakes, OR major but not frequent mistakes, which do not affect communication) – partly fluent speech (with minor and frequent disturbances in the flow of speech) and comprehensible pronunciation (with minor frequent mistakes)
1–4 marks (fail)	– partial or unclear communication of information suggested in the bullet points – basic (or non-existent) grammatical and lexical structures (with major or frequent mistakes which often disturb communication) – little or no fluency in speech (with major or frequent disturbances in the flow of speech) and/or incomprehensible pronunciation (with major or frequent mistakes – often changing the meaning of the words)

Photo Description Tasks

There are four Photo Description Tasks. We suggest students complete these tasks with the teacher. For each task, there is a list of additional questions based on the photo.

We suggest the following assessment criteria for the photo description tasks:

Assessment of the photo description tasks (10 marks)	
8–10 marks (very good)	– completely and clearly described photos with complete answers to all the questions asked by the teacher – varied grammatical and lexical structures (with minor but not frequent mistakes which do not disturb communication) – fluent speech (with minor disturbances in the flow of speech) and correct pronunciation (with minor mistakes)

4

5–7 marks (pass)	– mostly/partly clearly described photos and partial answers to most of the questions asked by the examiner – sufficient grammatical and lexical structures (with minor, frequent mistakes, OR major but not frequent mistakes, which do not disturb communication) – partly fluent speech (with minor and frequent disturbances in the flow of speech) and comprehensible pronunciation (with minor and frequent mistakes)
1–4 marks (fail)	– unclear or non-existent photo description and partial or non-existent answers to all/majority of the questions asked by the teacher – basic (or non-existent) grammatical and lexical structures (with major or frequent mistakes which often disturb communication) – little or no fluency in speech (with major or frequent disturbances in the flow of speech) and/or incomprehensible pronunciation (with major or frequent mistakes – often changing the meaning of the words)

Writing Tasks

There are six Writing Tasks in total – one for every unit in the Students' Book. Students can be asked to do the writing task at home or you can ask them to do it in class. Doing it in class means you can time students, which is important when preparing for exams. You can also monitor how students prepare for the task.

We suggest the following assessment criteria for the writing tasks:

Assessment of the writing tasks (10 marks)	
8–10 marks (very good)	– complete and clear communication of information suggested in the bullet points – varied grammatical and lexical structures (with minor but not frequent mistakes which do not affect comprehension) – fluent and cohesive text (with minor mistakes in punctuation, spelling and capitalisation)
5–7 marks (pass)	– mostly/partly clear communication of information suggested in the bullet points – sufficient grammatical and lexical structures (with minor, frequent mistakes, OR major but not frequent mistakes, which do not affect comprehension) – partly fluent and cohesive text (with minor, frequent mistakes, OR major but not frequent mistakes in punctuation, spelling and capitalisation of particular words and phrases)
1–4 marks (fail)	– partial or unclear communication of information suggested in the bullet points – basic (or non-existent) grammatical and lexical structures (with major or frequent mistakes which often disturb comprehension) – little or no fluency and cohesion in text (with major or frequent mistakes in punctuation, spelling and capitalisation of particular words and phrases – often changing the meaning of words)

Midyear Test

This covers the material from the first six units of the book. It is similar in structure to the Language and skills tests but longer (with a total of 60 marks compared to 50 marks). The Midyear Test is offered in only one version.

End of year Test

This covers material from all 12 units of the Students' Book. It is similar in structure to the Midyear test and is also offered in only one version.

Placement Tests

There is one Placement test included in this Test Book: *Elementary←→Pre-intermediate*. This test should be administered at the beginning of the school year to make sure the appropriate level of the Students' Book is selected. The *Real Life* Placement tests are designed to help the teacher to place students at the right level of the *Real Life* series. If students get less than sixty percent of the answers right, they should use the lower level (for example: the Elementary level in the case of the *Elementary←→Pre-intermediate* Placement Test). If they score more than seventy percent, we advise you to use the higher level (for example: the Pre-intermediate level in the case of the *Elementary←→Pre-Intermediate* Placement Test). Sixty to seventy percent of the right answers means your students are in the middle of the two levels and your decision where to place these students should depend on the level of the majority of students in the class.

Pass marks

Pass marks may vary between different institutions and on different types of tests/examinations. For the assessment in the *Real Life* coursebook, a guideline is that the pass mark for any test is fifty percent. The assessment tables for roleplays, photo description tasks and writing tasks indicate which marks merit a 'fail', 'pass' or 'very good' assessment of a student's abilities.

The majority of tests in *Real Life* are typical progress achievement tests, covering a relatively narrow range of lexical, grammatical and functional material. Therefore, a suggested pass mark might appear higher than on some official examinations, which test general language proficiency rather than the linguistic material covered during several weeks of teaching.

In everyday classroom assessment, the teacher can adjust the pass mark, lowering or raising it appropriately, depending on their school policy, students' entry level, the level of a particular group or for motivational and other reasons.

Name: ....

1 Choose the best word a, b or c to complete the sentences.

0   Your mother's mother is your _____ .
 (a) grandmother   b cousin   c wife

1   Tom's parents are very young: his mother is 35 and his _____ is 37.
 a husband   b uncle   c father

2   I've got one _____ and two brothers.
 a sister   b aunt   c wife

3   My father's brother is my_____.
 a uncle   b grandfather   c cousin

4   Mrs Brown has got one _____ and two sons.
 a child   b daughter   c sister

/2

2 Write in the missing letters *a, e, i, o, u* or *y* to complete the words.

0   a c o m p u t e r
1   a b _ c _ c l _
2   a m _ b _ l _ phone
3   a sk _ t _ b _ _ rd
4   k _ _ s
5   a w _ ll _ t
6   a packet of t _ s s _ _ s

/6

3 Complete the description with the words below.

short   beard   young ✔
friendly   fair

Georgia's ⁰ ___young___ – she's only nine years old. She's got long ¹ _____ hair.
She's very ² _____ . Georgia's father is about 35. He's got ³ _____ dark hair. He's got a ⁴ _____ .

/2

4 Write positive, negative and interrogative sentences with *have got*.

0   I/an MP3 player/in my bag (✔)
 ___I've got an MP3 player in my bag.___

1   Peter/a DVD player (✗)
 _____

2   We/three TVs/in our house (✔)
 _____

3   You/a boyfriend (?)
 _____

4   I/a moustache (✔)
 _____

/4

5 Complete the sentences with the correct form of *there is/there are*.

0   ___Are there___ three dogs in the photo?
1   _____ fifteen boys in my class.
2   _____ a pencil in your bag?
3   _____ two pens here. There's only one!

/3

6 Underline the correct word(s) to complete the sentences.

0   They've got three *child/children*.
1   His *grandparent's/grandparents'* names are Gill and David.
2   There are a lot of *person/people* in the street.
3   Where is *your/yours* skateboard?
4   Becky is *Tom's/Tom* girlfriend.
5   There is a *man/men* in the picture.
6   It's not Mark's computer, it's *our/ours*!

/3

Score: _____ /20 marks

6

Name: ....

1 Choose the best word a, b or c to complete the sentences.

0 Your mother's mother is your _____ .
 (a) grandmother b cousin   c wife

1 Ann's _____'s name is Robert. They've got two children.
 a brother   b husband   c cousin

2 My mother's sister is my _____ .
 a father   b uncle   c aunt

3 Mr Smith has got one _____ and three daughters.
 a son   b brother   c child

4 Robert's _____ are quite old: his mother is 85 and his father is 90.
 a parents   b children   c cousins

/2

2 Write in the missing letters *a, e, i, o, u* or *y* to complete the words.

0 a c o m p u t e r
1 a c _ m _ r _
2 a games c _ n s _ l _
3 a g _ _ t _ r
4 _ _ r p h _ n _ s
5 a m _ r r _ r
6 a packet of c h _ w _ n g gum

/6

3 Complete the description with the words below.

| short | moustache | young ✔ |
| fair | shy | |

Jane's **0** _young_ – she's only 12 years old.
She's got **1** _____ dark hair. She's very
2 _____ . Jane's brother is 20. He's got long
3 _____ hair. He's got a **4** _____ .

/2

4 Write positive, negative and interrogative sentences with *have got*.

0 I/an MP3 player/in my bag (✔)
 I've got an MP3 player in my bag.

1 Robert/a beard (✗)
 _____

2 They/two DVD players/in their house (✔)
 _____

3 I/a skateboard (✗)
 _____

4 You/a girlfriend (?)
 _____

/4

5 Complete the sentences with the correct form of *there is/there are*.

0 _Are there_ three dogs in the photo?
1 _____ two pencils here. There's only one!
2 _____ fourteen girls in my class.
3 _____ a lip salve in your bag?

/3

6 Underline the correct word(s) to complete the sentences.

0 They've got three *child/children*.
1 This hairbrush isn't Fiona's. It's *my/mine*!
2 Matthew is *Olivia's/Olivia* boyfriend.
3 It's *their/theirs* computer.
4 There are five *woman/women* in my family.
5 His best *friend's/friends'* names are Chris and Ian.
6 There's one *person/people* in the picture.

/3

Score: _____ /20 marks

Name: ....

1 Match the verbs 1–6 with the correct word(s) a–g.

0	wake	*e*	a	to bed
1	do		b	books
2	wear		c	homework
3	go		d	at home
4	listen		e	up at 6 a.m.
5	read		f	to music
6	help		g	school uniform

/3

2 Write in the missing letters to complete the names of school subjects.

0 M *a t h s*

1 H _ _ _ _ _ y

2 F _ _ _ _ _ n Languages

3 S _ _ _ _ _ e

4 M _ _ _ c

5 Information and Communication
   T _ _ _ _ _ _ _ y (ICT)

/5

3 Choose the best word(s) a, b or c to complete the sentences.

0 Are these your new sunglasses? I like _____ .
   a their   (b) them   c they

1 Claire doesn't like Robert and she doesn't talk to _____ .
   a he   b his   c him

2 I _____ walk to school.
   a usually   b every day   c twice a week

3 _____ Imogen have Art on Mondays?
   a Does   b Is   c Has

4 Tell _____ what you want for breakfast.
   a I   b me   c my

5 They play football _____ .
   a always   b usually   c three times a month

6 We like Tom but he doesn't like _____ .
   a ours   b us   c our

/3

4 Write positive or negative sentences in the present simple.

0 Mr Perkins/teach/in our school (✗)
   Mr Perkins doesn't teach in our school.

1 She/get up/at 8 a.m. on Mondays (✔)
   _____

2 Robert's girlfriend/watch TV/every day (✔)
   _____

3 He/go to school/by bus (✗)
   _____

4 Hannah's brother/have lunch/at school (✔)
   _____

5 Mrs Smith/visit her grandmother/on Tuesdays (✗)
   _____

/5

5 Write questions for the answers.

0 *What music do you like?*
   I like dance music.

1 _____ ?
   They play tennis once a week.

2 _____ ?
   She wakes up at 10 a.m. on Sundays.

3 _____ ?
   GEOGRAPHY.

4 _____ ?
   I live in Katowice, in Poland.

/4

Score: _____ **/20 marks**

Name: ....

1 Match the verbs 1–6 with the correct word(s) a–g.

0 wake   *e*   a relatives
1 get   b sport
2 do   c TV
3 go   d for a walk
4 hang out   e up at 6 a.m.
5 visit   f with friends
6 watch   g dressed

/3

2 Write in the missing letters to complete the names of school subjects.

0 M *a t h s*
1 G _ _ _ _ _ _ _ y
2 D _ _ _ _ n and Technology
3 C _ _ _ z _ _ _ _ _ p
4 Physical E _ _ _ _ _ _ _ n (PE)
5 E _ _ _ _ _ h

/5

3 Choose the best word(s) a, b or c to complete the sentences.

0 Are these your new sunglasses? I like _____ .
  a their   (b) them   c they
1 I _____ listen to the radio in the morning.
  a often   b once a week
  c four times a month
2 Mrs Smith likes _____ but we don't like her.
  a our   b us   c ours
3 Where is Paul? I've got a packet of chewing gum for _____ .
  a he   b him   c his
4 _____ they have Art lessons in their school?
  a Do   b Are   c Have
5 We wear school uniform _____ .
  a always   b usually   c every day
6 Please call _____ tomorrow after school.
  a I   b my   c me

/3

4 Write positive or negative sentences in the present simple.

0 Mr Perkins/teach/in our school (✗)
  Mr Perkins doesn't teach in our school.
1 She/listen to music/every day (✗)
  _____
2 Tom/do his homework/at school (✔)
  _____
3 Our Maths lesson/start/at 11 a.m. (✗)
  _____
4 My brother/study/History (✔)
  _____
5 Joan/walk to school/with her best friend (✔)
  _____

/5

5 Write questions for the answers.

0 *What music do you like?*
  I like dance music.
1 _____ ?
  They go to the cinema every week.
2 _____ ?
  I have cereal for breakfast.
3 _____ ?
  Her parents work in London.
4 _____ ?
  Caroline usually gets up at 7 a.m.

/4

Score: _____ /20 marks

Unit 2

short test 2

Name: ....

1 Write the words below in the correct category.

> library   wardrobe   bedroom
> clothes shop   bathroom
> pharmacy   car park   post office
> armchair   greengrocer's   sink
> kitchen

Shops:

_____ , _____ , _____

Rooms in the house:

_____ , _____ , _____

Places in town:

_____ , _____ , _____

Things at home:

_____ , _____ , _____

/6

2 Write in the missing letters to complete the adjectives in each sentence.

0 My city has got f *a n t a s t i c* shops and department stores.

1 There are a lot of cars in my town and it's very p _ _ _ _ t _ _ .

2 The Museum of Science in London is g _ _ _ _ ! I often go there.

3 I like my city because it has got b _ _ u _ _ _ _ _ beaches and parks.

4 There are two i _ _ _ _ e _ _ _ _ _ museums in my town.

/4

3 Choose the best word a, b or c to complete the sentences.

0 We haven't got _____ shampoo.
   (a) any   b a   c some

1 Have you got _____ hairbrush?
   a some   b a   c any

2 There isn't _____ hot water.
   a a   b some   c any

3 There are _____ good films on TV.
   a some   b a   c any

4 Is there _____ traffic in your town?
   a any   b some   c a

/2

4 Underline the correct word(s) to complete the sentences.

0 I haven't got *many/much* time.

1 There aren't *much/many* cinemas in my town.

2 There's *much/a lot of* space in my room.

3 There isn't *much/many* traffic in my town.

4 How *much/many* money has he got?

5 Do you read *much/many* magazines?

6 I've got *much/a lot of* bags.

/3

5 Correct the mistake in each sentence.

0 I haven't got ~~some~~ money.
   I haven't got any money.

1 There's some park near my house – it's really nice!

_____

2 How much girls are there in your class?

_____

3 There isn't any TV in this room.

_____

4 There are much clothes in my wardrobe.

_____

5 There aren't some hotels in my town.

_____

/5

Score: _____ /20 marks

Name: ....

1 Write the words below in the correct category.

> carpet   cooker   bedroom
> living room   baker's   town hall
> kitchen   fire station   stadium
> bookshop   basin   newsagent's

Places in town:

_____ , _____ , _____

Things at home:

_____ , _____ , _____

Rooms in the house:

_____ , _____ , _____

Shops:

_____ , _____ , _____

         /6

2 Write in the missing letters to complete the adjectives in each sentence.

0 My city has got f *antastic* shops and department stores.

1 The weather is t _ _ _ _ _ _ _ in my city. It's often cold and wet.

2 San Francisco has got a f _ _ _ _ _ bridge.

3 The Museum of Natural History in Chicago is b _ _ _ l _ _ _ _ ! I go there twice a year.

4 I love London because it's an _ x _ _ _ _ _ g multicultural city.

         /4

3 Choose the best word a, b or c to complete the sentences.

0 We haven't got _____ shampoo.

   (a) any   b a   c some

1 There are _____ great shops in my city.

   a a   b some   c any

2 Have you got _____ packet of tissues?

   a any   b some   c a

3 Are there _____ hotels in your town?

   a any   b a   c some

4 There isn't _____ sugar in my coffee.

   a a   b some   c any

         /2

4 <u>Underline</u> the correct word(s) to complete the sentences.

0 I haven't got *many/<u>much</u>* time.

1 There's *a lot of/much* furniture in my room.

2 There are *many/much* schools in this city.

3 Do you drink *much/many* cola?

4 We've got *much/a lot of* books in the bookcase.

5 We haven't got *much/many* money.

6 How *much/many* rooms are there in your flat?

         /3

5 Correct the mistake in each sentence.

0 I haven't got ~~some~~ money.

   I haven't got any money.

1 There is much space in my bedroom.

_____

2 There aren't some swimming pools in my town.

_____

3 There's some great market near my house – I often go there.

_____

4 Is there many rain in your city?

_____

5 We haven't got any washing machine in our house.

_____

         /5

Score: _____ /20 marks

Unit 3

short test 3

Name: ....

1 Choose the best word a, b or c to complete the sentences.

0 We _____ football every day.

   (**a**) play   **b** go   **c** do

1 We use a wetsuit for _____ .

   a rock climbing   **b** surfing   **c** running

2 I go to the mountains twice a year because I love _____ .

   a skiing   **b** gymnastics   **c** skateboarding

3 How often do you do _____ ?

   a baseball   **b** karate   **c** golf

4 I can't play _____ .

   a judo   **b** rowing   **c** basketball

/2

2 Rearrange the letters to find different parts of the body.

0 C E K N   _neck_

1 D A E H   _____

2 R A M   _____

3 G F R N I E   _____

4 E N K E   _____

5 O F T O   _____

/5

3 Write in the missing letters to complete the words in each sentence.

0 I often feel s _i c k_ in the car.

1 I've got a t _ _ _ _ _ c _ _ – one of my teeth hurts.

2 Steven feels terrible. He's got a cold and a c _ _ _ _ .

3 I can't run very well because I've got a s _ _ _ leg.

/3

4 Write positive, negative and interrogative sentences with *can*.

0 I/swim/very well (✔)

   I can swim very well.

1 Your brother/dance (?)

   _____

2 My sister/cycle/very well (✗)

   _____

3 They/play rugby/quite well (✔)

   _____

/3

5 Make adverbs from the adjectives below and complete the sentences. There are two words you do not need.

slow   quick ✓   easy   loud
happy   good   terrible
hard

0 Robert runs very _quickly_ . He's a very good sportsman.

1 Please, speak more _____ . I can't hear you.

2 My sister can't dance, she dances _____ .

3 Gill's parents work very _____ . They start work at 6 a.m. and finish at 6 p.m.

4 We drive very _____ in my town. There's a lot of traffic.

5 She's a good tennis player. She plays tennis _____ .

/5

6 Underline the correct word(s) to complete the sentences.

0 Please, _help_/you help me with my homework.

1 *No touch/Don't touch* it! It's mine!

2 You've got a stomachache? *Go/You go* to the doctor.

3 *Drink/Don't* drink a lot of cola. It's not good for you.

4 *Don't speak/Not speak* English to him. He doesn't understand.

/2

Score: _____ /20 marks

     PHOTOCOPIABLE   © Pearson Education Limited 2010

short test 4b   Unit 4

Name: ....

1 Choose the best word a, b or c to complete the sentence.

0 We _____ football every day.
   (a) play   b go   c do

1 You need a boat to go _____ .
   a rowing   b swimming   c running

2 How often does Nick do _____ ?
   a judo   b tennis   c basketball

3 I can't play _____ .
   a karate   b surfing   c volleyball

4 We use a rope for _____ .
   a skiing   b rock climbing
   c skateboarding

   /2

2 Rearrange the letters to find different parts of the body.

0 C E K N   _neck_
1 C A B K   _____
2 D S U H R O L E _____
3 O E W B L   _____
4 E G L   _____
5 O T E   _____

   /5

3 Write in the missing letters to complete the words in each sentence.

0 I often feel s _i c k_ in the car.
1 I've got a p _ _ _ in my knee and I can't run very well.
2 My back hurts – I've got b _ _ _ a _ _ _ .
3 Ruth doesn't feel well. She's got a c _ _ _ and a cough.

   /3

4 Write positive, negative and interrogative sentences with *can*.

0 I/swim/very well (✔)
   I can swim very well.

1 Bob and Tricia/dance/quite well (✔)
   _____

2 I/ride a horse/ well (✗)
   _____

3 Your girlfriend/play/computer games (?)
   _____

   /3

5 Make adverbs from the adjectives below and complete the sentences. There are two words you do not need.

| careful | quick ✓ | easy | quiet |
| clear | hard | terrible | fast |

0 Robert runs very _quickly_ . He's a very good sportsman.
1 Please, drive _____ . There's a lot of traffic on this road.
2 We've got a very good teacher. She always explains things _____ .
3 Peter is a very good swimmer. He swims very _____ .
4 Children, speak _____ , please. You're very loud.
5 My sister always makes friends _____ .

   /5

6 Underline the correct word(s) to complete the sentences.

0 Please, *help/you help* me with my homework.
1 You've got a stomachache? *Not eat/Don't eat* quickly.
2 *Watch/Don't watch* English films. It's very good for your English.
3 You are very tired? *Go/You go* to bed.
4 *Don't wait/Not wait* for me today after school.

   /2

Score: _____ /20 marks

Name: ....

1 Cross out the words that you cannot use with the word in bold.

0 **mix** them together/the potatoes and the milk/
~~the tomatoes on the salad~~

1 **boil** the potatoes/the lettuce/the eggs

2 **cut** the oil/the tomatoes/the apples

3 **put** the olives into a salad bowl/the tuna on top/the green beans into pieces

/3

2 Write in the missing letters to complete the words in each sentence.

0 Tom is a vegetarian. He doesn't eat m _e_ _a_ _t_.

1 Tomatoes are my favourite v _ _ _ t _ _ _ _ .

2 I often drink orange j _ _ _ _ .

3 Don't eat so many _ r _ _ _ _ . Have an apple!

4 Do you want your meat with potatoes or r _ _ _ ?

5 I like all kinds of fruit but _ a _ _ n _ _ and apples are my favourite.

6 Do you have c _ _ _ _ _ for breakfast?

/6

3 Complete the sentences with the correct forms of the verbs in brackets.

0 I _like drinking_ (like/drink) cola.

1 Tom _____ (hate /watch) football on TV.

2 I _____ (not like/wear) school uniform.

3 _____ (they) (like/visit) relatives?

4 She _____ (love/hang out) with friends.

5 _____ (your sister) (like/go) to bed early?

/5

4 Choose the best answer a, b or c to complete the sentences.

0 My mother is _____ teacher.
(a) a   b –   c the

1 My father works at a post office. He walks to work because_____ post office is near our house.
a a   b –   c the

2 Do you like _____ cheese?
a the   b –   c a

3 My sister makes _____ salad twice a week.
a the   b a   c –

4 I don't really like _____ olives.
a –   b the   c an

/2

5 Correct the mistake in each sentence.

0 I often go for a walk with a̶ friends.
I often go for a walk with friends.

1 There is sofa in the living room.

_____

2 His wife is the chef and works in a restaurant.

_____

3 I never buy the clothes in a supermarket.

_____

4 My brother's a actor and my sister's a doctor.

_____

/4

Score: _____ /20 marks

Name: ....

1 Cross out the words that you cannot use with the word in bold.

0 **mix** them together/the lemon juice and the oil/~~the tomatoes on the salad~~

1 **put** the apples into pieces/the eggs on top/ the lettuce into a big bowl

2 **boil** the beans/the potatoes/the cheese

3 **cut** the onions/the juice/the bananas

/3

2 Write in the missing letters to complete the words in each sentence.

0 Tom is a vegetarian. He doesn't eat m_e_ _a_ _t_.

1 My little brother always drinks m_ _ _ in the morning.

2 We usually have meat or f _ _ _ for dinner.

3 Don't eat so many _ i _ _u _ _ _ !

4 Many people eat _e _ _ _ l for breakfast.

5 I like apples and bananas. They're my favourite types of f _ _ _ _.

6 On Fridays I usually have a p_ _ _ _ for dinner.

/6

3 Complete the sentences with the correct forms of the verbs in brackets.

0 I _like drinking_ (like/drink) cola.

1 Mary _____ (love/cook) Chinese food.

2 _____ (your teacher/like/listen) to music?

3 We _____ (not like/help) at home.

4 _____ (they/like/watch) sport on TV?

5 I _____ (love/read) books about the past.

/5

4 Choose the best answer a, b or c to complete the sentences.

0 My mother is _____ teacher.
   (a) a   b –   c the

1 Gill doesn't like _____ ice-cream.
   a an   b –   c the

2 After school my boyfriend works in a music shop. He cycles to work because _____ music shop is only 500 metres from our school.
   a the   b –   c a

3 I don't really like _____ eggs.
   a the   b an   c –

4 Have _____ drink before you play tennis.
   a the   b –   c a

/2

5 Correct the mistake in each sentence.

0 I often go for a walk with a̶ friends.
   I often go for a walk with friends.

1 I have a sandwich and a apple for lunch.
   _____

2 I often buy the magazines at a newsagent's.
   _____

3 There is cooker in the kitchen.
   _____

4 Her husband's the doctor and works in a hospital.
   _____

/4

Score: _____ /20 marks

Unit 5

short test 5

Name: ....

1 Read the sentences. Tick (✔) true or cross (✗) false.

0 A scarf is a kind of shirt. [✗]
1 Trainers are a kind of trousers. [ ]
2 Earrings are a kind of jewellery. [ ]
3 People wear sweaters when it's hot. [ ]
4 You wear a hat on your head. [ ]

/2

2 Complete the sentences with one word in each gap.

0 How often do you s*urf*_____ the internet?
1 First type in your username or p_____ .
2 I use instant messaging to c_____ with my friends.
3 Many people create their own web p_____ or write their own blogs.
4 Do you often d_____ music or games from the internet?
5 How many emails do you s_____ a day?
6 I do many things o_____: I use instant messaging, read blogs and buy books.

/6

3 Put the words in the correct order to make sentences.

0 music/I/listening/to/am/
   I am listening to music.
1 Sam?/to/are/writing/you/
   _____
2 for/they/waiting/the teacher/not/are/
   _____
3 drinking?/is/what/Nick/
   _____
4 running/very fast/Dave/and/Ian/are/
   _____

/4

4 Underline the correct word/s to complete the sentences.

0 I wear/*am wearing* a blue shirt today.
1 What do you do/are you doing here? It's very late. Go to bed now!
2 How often do you walk/are you walking to school?
3 You can talk loudly. The baby's not sleeping/doesn't sleep.
4 We usually have/are having cereal for breakfast.

/2

5 Put the verbs in brackets into the correct tense. Use the present simple or the present continuous.

0 She ___*is getting*___ (get) dressed now.
1 We usually _____ (go) to bed at 11 p.m.
2 They _____ (wear) school uniform to school.
3 She can't help you now. She _____ (peel) the potatoes for lunch.
4 I'm very busy at the moment. I _____ (study) for my History test.
5 _____ (they/talk) to Mr Smith? I can't see very well.
6 Elizabeth _____ (not/play) volleyball well.

/6

Score: _____ /20 marks

Name: ....

1 Read the sentences. Tick (✔) true or cross (✗) false.

0 A scarf is a kind of shirt.   [✗]
1 Some people wear jeans with a belt.   [ ]
2 Boots are a kind of shoe.   [ ]
3 People wear T-shirts when it's very cold. [ ]
4 A jacket is a kind of skirt.   [ ]

/2

2 Complete the sentences with one word in each gap.

0 How often do you s*urf*_____ the internet?
1 Can you c_____ your own web page?
2 Do you use instant m_____ to chat with your friends?
3 I can't l_____ on because I don't remember my password.
4 Sandra writes her own b_____ . You can go online and read about her life.
5 First you need to type in your u_____ or password.
6 I often use the internet to do r_____ for my school projects.

/6

3 Put the words in the correct order to make sentences.

0 music/I/listening/to/am/
  I am listening to music.

1 Jessica/what/eating?/is/
  _____

2 are /very loudly/Georgia/singing/and/Beth/
  _____

3 talking/me?/are/to/you/
  _____

4 not/we/Luke/are/to/listening/
  _____

/4

4 Underline the correct word(s) to complete the sentences.

0 I *wear/am wearing* a blue shirt today.
1 We can talk if you want. I'*m not doing/don't do* my homework now.
2 They never *cycle/are cycling* to school.
3 What *are you reading/do you read*? Is it interesting?
4 How often *do you eat/are you eating* pizza?

/2

5 Put the verbs in brackets into the correct tense. Use the present simple or the present continuous.

0 She ___*is getting*___ (get) dressed now.
1 Andrew often _____ (have) a sandwich for lunch.
2 I _____ (go) to bed now. I'm very tired.
3 Mark _____ (not like) meat.
4 They _____ (play) tennis now.
5 Frank's busy at the moment. He _____ (talk) on the phone.
6 On Saturdays we never _____ (wake) up before 9 a.m.

/6

Score: _____ /20 marks

Unit 6

short test 6

Name: ....

1 Write in the missing letters to complete the names of five types of music.

0 p u n k
1 r _ _ _
2 f _ _ _
3 c _ _ _ s _ _ _ _
4 d _ _ _ _
5 h _ _ - h _ _

/5

2 Read the sentences. Tick (✔) true or cross (✗) false.

0 A festival is a special day. ✔
1 Candles are a kind of food. ☐
2 People watch fireworks in the evening or at night. ☐
3 A parade is a kind of sweet. ☐
4 People give presents on special occasions. ☐

/2

3 Write positive, negative and interrogative sentences with the verb *be* in the past simple tense.

0 Mr Macey/in Paris/last year (✔)
   Mr Macey was in Paris last year.
1 The weather/terrible/yesterday (✔)
   _____
2 Where/Paul and John/last night (?)
   _____
3 We/tired/after our PE lesson (✗)
   _____
4 the concert/good (?)
   _____

/4

4 Put the verbs below in the correct column and write their past simple forms.

sing ✔   dance ✔   go   wear
celebrate   cook

Regular verbs

infinitive	past simple form
dance	*danced*
_____	_____
_____	_____

Irregular verbs

infinitive	past simple form
sing	*sang*
_____	_____
_____	_____

/4

5 Complete the sentences with the past simple form of the verbs below.

send   give   watch ✔   stay
have   start

0 I *watched* a very interesting film last night.
1 The party _____ at 6 p.m.
2 I _____ a terrible headache yesterday.
3 They _____ us a card for Christmas.
4 We _____ in bed very late last Sunday.
5 My father _____ me £100 two weeks ago.

/5

Score: _____ /20 marks

Name: ....

1 Write in the missing letters to complete the names of five types of music.

0 p u n k
1 j _ _ _
2 p _ _
3 h _ _ _ _ m _ _ _ _
4 _ l _ _ _ c _ _
5 d _ _ _ _

/5

2 Read the sentences. Tick (✔) true or cross (✗) false.

0 A festival is a special day. ✓
1 Sweets are special clothes. ☐
2 You can watch fireworks in the morning. ☐
3 In many countries people send cards on special occasions. ☐
4 Candles give light. ☐

/2

3 Write positive, negative and interrogative sentences with the verb *be* in the past simple tense.

0 Mr Macey/in Paris/last year (✔)
  Mr Macey was in Paris last year.
1 Where/you/last Monday (?)
  _____
2 Her cousins/friendly (✗)
  _____
3 the film/interesting (?)
  _____
4 I/at the cinema/last weekend (✔)
  _____

/4

4 Put the verbs below in the correct column and write their past simple forms.

sing ✓   dance ✓   decorate
give   start   have

Regular verbs

infinitive	past simple form
dance	danced
_____	_____
_____	_____

Irregular verbs

infinitive	past simple form
sing	sang
_____	_____
_____	_____

/4

5 Complete the sentences with the past simple form of the verbs below.

finish   tidy   watch ✔   go
put   wear

0 I _watched_ a very interesting film last night.
1 We _____ to London in January.
2 The party _____ at 12 p.m.
3 I _____ your book on the table.
4 Sandra _____ a beautiful black dress yesterday.
5 They _____ their rooms last week.

/5

Score: _____ /20 marks

Unit 7

short test 7

Name: ....

1 Write in the missing letters *a, e, i, o, u* or *y* to complete the names of electrical objects.

0 a m _o_ b _i_ l _e_ phone
1 a h _ _ r d r _ _ r
2 a c _ _ k _ r
3 an MP3 p l _ _ _ r
4 a mobile phone c h _ r g _ r
5 an electric k _ t t l _

/5

2 Choose the best word a, b or c to complete the sentences.

0 Who _____ the Golden Gate Bridge in San Francisco?
   (a) designed   **b** invented   **c** discovered
1 Nowadays people can travel _____ to many places.
   a useful   **b** easily   **c** convenient
2 Who _____ antibiotics?
   a invented   **b** designed   **c** discovered
3 Electricity changed the _____ we live.
   a way   **b** life   **c** world
4 You need _____ to wake you up in the morning.
   a a toaster   **b** an alarm clock
   c an electric toothbrush

/2

3 Change the sentences into negative or *yes/no* questions in the past simple.

0 I enjoyed the party yesterday. (✗)
   I didn't enjoy the party yesterday.
1 They went to the cinema last weekend. (?)
   _____
2 Becky and Helen had a good time on holiday. (?)
   _____
3 We ate pizza yesterday. (✗)
   _____
4 Your cousin sent you an email last week. (?)
   _____
5 I saw our English teacher at school yesterday. (✗)
   _____
6 The children woke up very late on Saturday. (✗)
   _____

/6

4 Write questions in the past simple. Choose the question words from the box.

> what ✓   where   when   what
> who   how many

0 _What did Charlie want?_
   Charlie wanted some milk.
1 _____
   He wore jeans and a T-shirt.
2 _____
   They went to the USA.
3 _____
   She visited her best friend.
4 _____
   I read three books.
5 _____
   They finished work in the evening.

/5

5 Underline the correct word(s) to complete the sentences.

0 Where *did you buy/you bought* your earrings?
1 Who *created/did create* the World Wide Web?
2 What *invented Laszlo Biro/did Laszlo Biro invent*?
3 Who *closed/did close* the door?
4 Who *did you go/you went* to lunch with yesterday?

/2

Score: _____ /20 marks

PHOTOCOPIABLE   © Pearson Education Limited 2010

Name: ....

1 Write in the missing letters *a, e, i, o, u* or *y* to complete the names of electrical objects.

0 a m _o_ b _i_ l _e_ phone

1 a t _ _ st _ r

2 a mobile phone c h _ r g _ r

3 a r _ d _ _

4 an _ l _ rm clock

5 an electric t _ _ t h b r _ sh

               /5

2 Choose the best word a, b or c to complete the sentences.

0 Who _____ the Golden Gate Bridge in San Francisco?

  (a) designed   **b** invented   **c** discovered

1 My new mobile phone is very _____ to use.

  a imaginary   **b** easy   **c** useful

2 The internet changed the _____ we live.

  a world   **b** life   **c** way

3 Who _____ the mobile phone?

  a invented   **b** discovered   **c** built

4 You need _____ to boil water for tea.

  a a hairdryer   **b** an MP3 player
  c an electric kettle

               /2

3 Change the sentences into negative or *yes/no* questions in the past simple.

0 I enjoyed the party yesterday. (✗)

  I didn't enjoy the party yesterday.

1 I made breakfast for my family yesterday. (✗)

  _____

2 Sam rode his bicycle to school on Monday. (?)

  _____

3 We watched the match on TV last night. (✗)

  _____

4 You went to school yesterday. (?)

  _____

5 Peter's parents sold their house last year. (?)

  _____

6 I texted my boyfriend at the weekend. (✗)

  _____

               /6

4 Write questions in the past simple. Choose the question words from the box.

> what ✓   where   what time
> what   who   how many

0 *What did Charlie want?*

  Charlie wanted some milk.

1 _____

  I watched three films at the weekend.

2 _____

  They woke up at 8 a.m.

3 _____

  Sandra saw our Geography teacher yesterday.

4 _____

  John's grandparents lived in Argentina.

5 _____

  Mrs Smith gave me a scarf.

               /5

5 Underline the correct word(s) to complete the sentences.

0 Where *did you buy/you bought* your earrings?

1 Who *did you meet/you met* on the way to school?

2 Who *opened/did open* the window?

3 What *designed Karl Benz/did Karl Benz design*?

4 Who *painted/did paint* The Sunflowers?

               /2

Score: _____ /20 marks

Name: ....

1 Write each word/expression below in the correct category.

> paper ✓   litter bins   plastic
> windy   pollution   floods ✓
> cycle lanes ✓   green spaces   warm ✓
> sunny   hurricanes   bottles

Weather: warm, _____

Environmental problems: floods, _____

_____

Recyclable rubbish: paper, _____

_____

Solutions to local problems: cycle lanes, _____

_____

/4

2 Correct the **underlined** word in each sentence.

0 It's very ~~hot~~ today. Take your sweater with you.
   _____cold_____

1 We often have <u>floods</u> here because there's no rain in this area. _____

2 I can't see the sun. It's very <u>stormy</u> today.

   _____

3 <u>Solar</u> warming is a big problem. _____

4 I think I am green – I always buy products with little or no <u>rubbish</u>. _____

/4

3 Put the adjectives in brackets into the comparative.

0 My computer is _more expensive_ (expensive) than yours.

1 Ruth is _____ (nice) than Angela.

2 The film is _____ (interesting) than the book.

3 Mark is _____ (bad) at tennis than you.

4 In my family I'm _____ (green) than my sister.

/4

4 Write sentences comparing the things below using the adjectives in bold.

0 a cooker/an electric kettle   **cheap**
   An electric kettle is cheaper than a cooker.

1 our teacher/my best friend   **tall**
   _____

2 History/Geography   **difficult**
   _____

3 apples/sweets   **healthy**
   _____

4 my mobile phone/my friend's mobile
   phone   **good**
   _____

/4

5 Put the words in the correct order to make predictions about the future.

0 to other planets/people/travel/in twenty years/will/.
   People will travel to other planets in
   twenty years.

1 tomorrow/sunny/it/be/won't/.

   _____

2 in/ten years?/where/you/will/be/

   _____

3 oil/there/the future/in/won't/be enough/.

   _____

4 the/of vegetables/next year/will/go down/price/.

   _____

/4

Score: _____ /20 marks

PHOTOCOPIABLE   © Pearson Education Limited 2010

Name: ....

1 Write each word/expression below in the correct category.

> paper ✓   droughts   traffic-free zones
> rainy   foggy   floods ✓
> public transport   packaging
> warm ✓   batteries   global warming
> cycle lanes ✓

Weather: warm, _____

Environmental problems: floods, _____
_____

Recyclable rubbish: paper, _____
_____

Solutions to local problems: cycle lanes, _____
_____

/4

2 Correct the <u>underlined</u> word in each sentence.

0 It's very ~~hot~~ today. Take your sweater with you.
   ___cold___

1 <u>Rainforests</u> have very strong winds.
   _____

2 We love the weather in July – it's very warm
   and <u>snowy</u>. _____

3 <u>Solar power</u> is a big problem in this area –
   there are a lot of cars and the air is very bad.
   _____

4 It's very easy to cycle in my city because we've
   got a lot of <u>litter bins</u>. _____

/4

3 Put the adjectives in brackets into the comparative.

0 My computer is *more expensive* (expensive) than yours.

1 I'm _____ (good) at swimming than you.

2 Is England _____ (big) than Scotland?

3 Water is _____ (polluted) in cities than in small villages.

4 My brother's bedroom is _____ (clean) than mine.

/4

4 Write sentences comparing the things below using the adjectives in bold.

0 a cooker/an electric kettle   **cheap**
   An electric kettle is cheaper than a cooker.

1 London/Paris   **beautiful**
   _____

2 my computer/my friend's computer   **bad**
   _____

3 Maths/Science   **easy**
   _____

4 my best friend/our teacher   **short**
   _____

/4

5 Put the words in the correct order to make predictions about the future.

0 to other planets/people/travel/ in twenty years/will/.
   People will travel to other planets in
   twenty years.

1 be/it/stormy/won't/tomorrow/.
   _____

2 next year/the/of clothes/go up/will /price/.
   _____

3 rain/there/won't/the future/be much/in/.
   _____

4 where/live/she/in/five years?/will/
   _____

/4

Score: _____ /20 marks

Name: ....

1 <u>Underline</u> the correct word to complete the sentences.

0 My father goes to work <u>by</u>/on car.
1 I often travel by/on train.
2 My sister always goes to school by/on foot.
3 We went to the city centre by/on bus.
4 They went to Australia by/on ship.

/2

2 Write in the missing letters to complete the words in each category.

Types of holiday: *beach*, s _ _ _ _ _ e _ _ _ _
Places to stay: *hotel*, holiday a _ _ _ _ _ _ _ t
Transport: *motorbike*, h _ _ _ c _ _ _ _ _

/3

3 Read the sentences. Tick (✔) true or cross (✗) false.

0 A moped is a kind of motorcycle. ✔
1 A campsite is a type of holiday. ☐
2 A kayak goes in the water. ☐
3 A bed and breakfast is a kind of meal. ☐
4 An adventure holiday is very active. ☐

/2

4 Write positive, negative and interrogative sentences with *be going to*.

0 Our teacher/give us/a lot of homework (✔)
Our teacher's going to give us a lot of homework.
1 We/play football/tomorrow after school (✔)
_____
2 What/you/do/at the weekend (?)
_____
3 I/go to the mountains/this winter (✗)
_____
4 Tom and Robert/come to my birthday party/ next Saturday (✗)
_____
5 Sarah/visit her grandmother/in hospital/ today (?)
_____

/5

5 Put the adjectives in brackets into the superlative.

0 What is the _cheapest_ (cheap) train ticket to London?
1 Who is _____ (tall) person in your family?
2 Maria's _____ (pretty) girl in my class.
3 Venice is _____ (beautiful) city I know.
4 A box of chocolates is _____ (good) present for my mother.

/4

6 Write questions with superlatives using the prompts and the adjectives in bold.

0 polluted city/in your country **polluted**
What's the most polluted city in your country?
1 film/you watched on TV last week **bad**
_____
2 actor/in your country **popular**
_____
3 room/in your house **small**
_____
4 car/in the world **expensive**
_____

/4

Score: _____ /20 marks

Name: ....

1 <u>Underline</u> the correct word to complete the sentences.

0 My father goes to work *by*/on car.

1 They went on a short trip *by*/on pedal boat.

2 My sister wants to travel around Scotland *by*/on motorbike.

3 Do you sometimes go to work *by*/on foot?

4 They got to the top of the mountain *by*/on helicopter.

/2

2 Write in the missing letters to complete the words in each category.

Transport: *bus*, s _ _ _

Places to stay: *hotel*, c _ _ _ _ _ e

Types of holiday: *walking*, a _ _ _ _ t _ _ _

/3

3 Read the sentences. Tick true (✔) or cross (✗) false.

0 A moped is a kind of motorcycle. ✔

1 Trains travel on water. ☐

2 A bed and breakfast is a place to stay on holiday. ☐

3 Canoes travel in the air. ☐

4 Camping is a type of holiday. ☐

/2

4 Write positive, negative and interrogative sentences with *be going to*.

0 Our teacher/give us/a lot of homework (✔)

Our teacher's going to give us a lot of homework.

1 I/study for my History test/at the weekend (✔)

_____

2 Georgia and Debbie/go to the cinema with us/next Friday (✗)

_____

3 Tom/play basketball with us/today after school (?)

_____

4 We/watch TV/this evening (✗)

_____

5 What time/you/get up/tomorrow (?)

_____

/5

5 Put the adjectives in brackets into the superlative.

0 What is the ___cheapest___ (cheap) train ticket to London?

1 Which is _____ (hot) month in your country?

2 Robert's _____ (intelligent) person I know.

3 What's _____ (busy) day of the week for you?

4 Henry's _____ (bad) student in my class.

/4

6 Write questions with superlatives using the prompts and the adjectives in bold.

0 polluted city/in your country   **polluted**

What's the most polluted city in your country?

1 place/you know   **beautiful**

_____

2 person/in your family   **happy**

_____

3 singer/in the world   **good**

_____

4 film/you watched on TV last week **interesting**

_____

/4

Score: _____ /20 marks

Name: ....

1 Match the verbs (1–6) with the correct expressions (a–g).

0 wear *e*   a polite
1 talk   b a good sense of humour
2 look   c at the weekend
3 have   d after people
4 be   e a uniform
5 sell   f on the phone
6 work   g things

/3

2 Complete the sentences with one word in each gap.

0 I'm very t *i r e d*. I'm going to go to bed early tonight.
1 I want to be a v _ _ in the future. I love animals.
2 My best friend has a very good _e _ _ _ _ – she remembers everything.
3 Olivia always keeps her things tidy. She's very o _ g _ _ _ _ _ _ .
4 My sister works in a shop. She's a shop a _ _ _ _ t _ _ _ .
5 You look very w _ _ _ _ _ _. What's the problem?
6 My sister works at the hospital. She's a _u_ _ _ .

/6

3 Complete the sentences with the adjectives below.

angry ✓   patient   reliable
surprised   happy

0 My mother was very ___*angry*___ yesterday because I didn't help her at home.
1 I'm really _____ that John is playing football this afternoon. He was very tired this morning.
2 Robert is not very _____ . He is always late for school.
3 I'm so _____ ! It's Saturday tomorrow and we don't have to go to school.
4 My sister is not very _____ . She doesn't like waiting for things!

/2

4 Complete the sentences with *in*, *on* or *at*.

0 We went to Spain ___*in*___ July.
1 We always start school _____ 9 o'clock.
2 I was born _____ 1 March.
3 Patricia didn't go to school _____ Monday.
4 I don't really like working _____ night.
5 _____ the morning, we went swimming.
6 Put your books _____ the table.
7 My sister lives _____ London.
8 I met her _____ the cinema.

/4

5 Complete the sentences with *have to* and the verbs in brackets.

0 You _____*have to go*_____ (go) to bed now. It's very late.
1 She _____ (get up) very early every day.
2 (you/send) _____ an email to your teacher today?
3 My little brother _____ (not help) at home.
4 They _____ (not wear) a uniform to school.
5 Mum, (I/do) _____ it now? I'm watching TV.

/5

Score: _____ /20 marks

Name: ....

1 Match the verbs (1–6) with the correct expressions (a–g).

0	wear	*e*	a	after people
1	have		b	a good memory
2	look		c	good at Maths
3	be		d	with money
4	work		e	a uniform
5	take		f	the guitar
6	play		g	photos

/3

2 Complete the sentences with one word in each gap.

0 I'm very t _i r e d_. I'm going to go to bed early tonight.

1 What's wrong Tom? Why are you so u _ _ _ _?

2 My father works in a bank. He's a bank c _ _ _ _ .

3 I'm always very n _ _ _ _ _ _ before my exams.

4 Peter wants to be a police _ _ _ i _ _ _ in the future.

5 Jane has a very good _ _ n _ _ of humour. She's fun to be with.

6 My little brother loves cars and wants to be a bus _r _ _ _ _ in the future.

/6

3 Complete the sentences with the adjectives below.

angry ✓   polite   bored   sad
independent

0 My mother was very _angry_ yesterday because I didn't help her at home.

1 I'm really _____ . There aren't any good films on TV and I have nothing to do.

2 Hannah's cousin is very _____ . She's two years old but she can get dressed and eat without help.

3 My sister is very _____ . She always says 'thank you' and 'please'.

4 You're very _____ today, Jack. Is everything alright?

/2

4 Complete the sentences with *in*, *on* or *at*.

0 We went to Spain _in_ July.

1 I always do my homework _____ the evening.

2 You're very good _____ tennis!

3 They came back from holiday _____ 26 August.

4 I can't read and listen to music _____ the same time.

5 What's _____ TV tonight?

6 My father finishes work _____ five o'clock.

7 My mobile phone is _____ my bag.

8 I didn't see them _____ Sunday.

/4

5 Complete the sentences with *have to* and the verbs in brackets.

0 You _have to go_ (go) to bed now. It's very late.

1 How much (you/pay) _____ for the bus?

2 I _____ (not work) at the weekend. I work Monday to Friday.

3 She _____ (help) at home and tidy her room every Saturday.

4 (we/read) _____ this book for tomorrow?

5 Robert _____ (not share) his bedroom with his older brother.

/5

Score: _____ /20 marks

Name: ....

1 Complete the sentences with the verbs below.

> have ✓　organise　greet
> receive　vote

0　On Saturdays, we usually ____*have*____ a meal in a restaurant.

1　The Japanese bow to _____ people.

2　Do many people _____ in the elections in your country?

3　Every year I _____ a lot of gifts for my birthday.

4　My teachers often _____ special events at school.

/2

2 Write in the missing letters to complete the words in each sentence.

0　How many p o l i t i c i a n s are there in the government in your country?

1　We wrote a letter to a member of the national g _ _ _ r _ _ _ _ _ .

2　In some countries, it's not nice to b _ _ _ your nose in public.

3　Obama won the election in 2008 and all his v _ _ _ _ _ were very happy.

4　Drugs and knife c _ _ _ _ are problems in some towns and cities.

5　Yesterday, Robert made a s _ _ _ _ _ about global warming. Everybody listened carefully.

/5

3 Put the verbs below in the correct column and write their past participles.

> see ✓　clean ✓　drive　talk
> think　help

Regular verbs

infinitive	past participle
clean	*cleaned*
_____	_____
_____	_____

Irregular verbs

infinitive	past participle
see	*seen*
_____	_____
_____	_____

/4

4 Write negative and interrogative sentences in the present perfect.

0　you/ever/write/a love letter (?)

Have you ever written a love letter?

1　Robert/never/win/any tennis matches (–)

_____

2　Hannah and Bethany/ever/download/music from the internet (?)

_____

3　I/never/visit/my aunt in Germany (–)

_____

4　Sue/ever/be/to Mexico (?)

_____

5　you/never/play/rugby (–)

_____

/5

5 Match the words (1–4) with the words (a–e) to make instructions or advice with *if* + imperative.

0　have a cold　*c*　　a　not go to bed late
1　be hungry　　　　b　say hello to her
2　feel tired　　　　c　not go out
3　see Joan tomorrow　d　not forget his birthday next week
4　like Peter　　　　e　eat an apple

0　*c If you have a cold, don't go out.*
1　_____
2　_____
3　_____
4　_____

/4

Score: _____ /20 marks

Name: ....

1 Complete the sentences with the verbs below.

> have ✓   blow   make   bow
> offer

0 On Saturdays, we usually ___*have*___ a meal in a restaurant.

1 Some people think it's not nice to _____ your nose in public.

2 If you _____ a gift in my country, people may give you something in return.

3 The Japanese _____ when they meet people.

4 Did you _____ a speech at school yesterday?

/2

2 Write in the missing letters to complete the words in each sentence.

0 How many p o l i t i c i a n s are there in the government in your country?

1 We p _ _ _ _ _ _ _ _ about the problems of bullying at our school.

2 Did Sandra r _ _ _ _ _ _ many gifts for Christmas?

3 B _ _ _ y _ _ _ at school and knife crime are serious problems for young people today.

4 My father wrote a letter to a member of the local _ o _ _ _ _ m _ _ _ .

5 Did you vote in the last e _ _ _ _ _ _ _ _ ?

/5

3 Put the verbs below in the correct column and write their past participles.

> see ✓   clean ✓   speak   want
> wear   sign

Regular verbs

infinitive	past participle
clean	*cleaned*
_____	_____
_____	_____

Irregular verbs

infinitive	past participle
see	*seen*
_____	_____
_____	_____

/4

4 Write negative and interrogative sentences in the present perfect.

0 you/ever/write/a love letter (?)
   Have you ever written a love letter?

1 your parents/ever/be/to San Francisco (?)
   _____

2 I/never/cycle/to school (–)
   _____

3 Mrs Brown/ever/walk/to work (?)
   _____

4 Chris/never/swim/in the sea (–)
   _____

5 you/ever/cook/lunch for your family (–)
   _____

/5

5 Match the words (1–4) with the words (a–e) to make instructions or advice with *if* + imperative.

0 have a cold c   a put on a sweater
1 see Paul tomorrow   b not give your real
                            name and address
2 be cold   c not go out
3 have a pain in your leg d invite him to my
                            birthday party
4 chat on the internet   e not play football

0 *c If you have a cold, don't go out.*
1 _____
2 _____
3 _____
4 _____

/4

Score: _____ /20 marks

Name: ....

Vocabulary & Grammar

1 Write each word/expression below in the correct category.

> Maths   parents   ICT   shy
> aunt   good-looking   keys
> Citizenship   tall   mirror
> husband   packet of tissues

My family:

_____ , _____ , _____

My things:

_____ , _____ , _____

School subjects:

_____ , _____ , _____

Describing people:

_____ , _____ , _____

/6

2 Complete the sentences with a verb in each gap.

0 On Sunday mornings, I ____*get*____ up at 9 o'clock.

1 Do you cycle to school or _____ ?

2 They never _____ to pop music.

3 I always _____ breakfast before school.

4 What time do you _____ to sleep?

5 We _____ TV every day.

/5

3 Put the words in the correct order to make present simple sentences.

0 his relatives/every/David/week/visits/.

   David visits his relatives every week.

1 friends?/you/how often/hang out/do/with/

   _____

2 goes/mother/once/shopping/a week/my/.

   _____

3 breakfast/get/I/after/dressed/usually/.

   _____

4 help/home/sister/at/my/doesn't/.

   _____

/4

4 Underline the correct word(s) to complete the sentences.

0 Georgia *have/has* got a new mobile phone.

1 Their *child/children* are very nice.

2 *Have/Do* you got a hairbrush in your bag?

3 These earphones are not Tom's! They're *my/mine*!

4 *Sandra's/Sandras'* grandmother lives in Italy.

5 *There are/There is* two computers in my room.

6 Tell *him /his* about your new girlfriend.

/3

5 Correct the mistake in each sentence.

0 I not like computer games.

   I don't like computer games.

1 What time she wake up?

   _____

2 There are three woman in my family.

   _____

3 My best friend doesn't got an mobile phone.

   _____

4 Do your sister often talk with her friends?

   _____

/4

6 Choose the best word a, b or c to complete the text.

My best friend Anna has got a ⁰ _____ and a sister. Her ¹ _____ name's Rachel. I like Rachel very much because she's very ² _____ . She's got short ³ _____ hair and she's very pretty. Anna and Rachel often ⁴ _____ sport. They love ⁵ _____ PE lessons at school. But they ⁶ _____ like Design and Technology.

0 a uncle	(b) brother	c aunt
1 a sister	b sister's	c sisters'
2 a friendly	b dark	c long
3 a fair	b slim	c fun
4 a have	b do	c go
5 a theirs	b them	c their
6 a aren't	b haven't	c don't

/3

Reading

7 Read the text and tick (✔) true or cross (✗) false.

1 Anna lives in Wales. ☐

2 Maggie isn't 16 years old. ☐

3 Anna has got four animals. ☐

4 Anna's favourite pop group is from Ireland. ☐

5 Kate usually does her homework before school in the morning. ☐

6 Anna has photos of her friends on her mobile phone. ☐

7 There is a picture of Anna's aunt on her mobile. ☐

8 Aunt Teresa visits Anna's family at the weekend. ☐

/8

home	browse	find	forum	music	video

My name is Anna and I live in Cardiff, the capital city of Wales. I am 16 years old and I have got two young sisters: Kate and Maggie. I have also got two dogs and a cat: the dogs are called Fido and Rex and the cat is called Masha.

Kate loves playing the guitar and Maggie loves singing. She often sings at family parties. I listen to music every day. My favourite pop group is The Corrs. The Corrs are an Irish band. I like their songs very much and I have got all their CDs. I also like Irish folk music. I go to Irish dancing classes on Mondays and Wednesdays.

After school, Maggie often reads her books and Kate usually does her homework. At the weekend, we usually hang out with friends or go to the cinema together. We sometimes watch DVDs.

I have got photos of my family on my mobile phone. I have a nice photo of my favourite relative, my Aunt Teresa. She visits us every Sunday and we sometimes play tennis together. She's very friendly and she's fun!

Do you think we can make friends? If you do, then write to me soon.

Listening

8 ⟨2⟩ Listen and match the speakers with the topics.

1 Alex   a work
2 Frank   b food
3 Gina   c free time
4 Martha d daily routine

/4

9 ⟨2⟩ Listen again and answer the questions.

1 What time does Alex usually meet with Jack?
_____

2 How does Frank go to work?
_____

3 What does Gina do after dinner?
_____

4 What does Martha do in her office?
_____

/4

Communication

10 Complete the sentences with a word in each gap.

1 A: _____ is my wife, Gina.
  B: Pleased to _____ you.

2 A: _____ are you from?
  B: From Berlin _____ Germany.

3 Dear Ann,
  How are you? I _____ you are well.

4 A: Is this your _____ time in the UK?
  B: No, it isn't.

5 That's all for now. See you _____ .
  Love,
  Jessie

6 A: What's your _____ football team?
  B: Manchester United, of _____ .

/9

Marks	
Vocabulary and grammar	/25 marks
Reading	/8 marks
Listening	/8 marks
Communication	/9 marks
Total:	**/50 marks**

Units 1&2   language and skills test 1a

Name: ....

Vocabulary & Grammar

1 Write each word/expression below in the correct category.

> uncle   slim   sunglasses
> Design and Technology   PE   wallet
> friendly   daughter   short
> Geography   wife   lip salve

Describing people:

_____ , _____ , _____

My things:

_____ , _____ , _____

My family:

_____ , _____ , _____

School subjects:

_____ , _____ , _____   /6

2 Complete the sentences with a verb in each gap.

0 On Sunday mornings, I _____*get*_____ up at 9 o'clock.

1 I always _____ my homework after school.

2 My mother doesn't _____ books – she hasn't got time.

3 What time do you usually _____ to bed?

4 On Mondays, I _____ lunch at school.

5 We _____ sport after school.   /5

3 Put the words in the correct order to make present simple sentences.

0 his relatives/every/David/week/visits/.
   David visits his relatives every week.

1 a month/the cinema/twice/to/goes/she/.

   _____

2 doesn't/uniform/brother/her/school/wear/.

   _____

3 to school/they/by bus?/go/how often/do/

   _____

4 friends/I/with/often/my/hang out/.

   _____   /4

4 Underline the correct word(s) to complete the sentences.

0 Georgia *have/has* got a new mobile phone.

1 Are these *your/yours* sunglasses?

2 Tell *our/us* about your new friends.

3 This is my *grandparent's/grandparents'* house.

4 Robert's *child/children* is very pretty.

5 *Do/Have* they got a new TV?

6 *Is there/Are there* a pen in your bag?   /3

5 Correct the mistake in each sentence.

0 I not like computer games.
   I don't like computer games.

1 We don't got a pet.

   _____

2 Do your sister often help at home?

   _____

3 When Tom listen to music?

   _____

4 There is a men in the park.

   _____   /4

6 Choose the best word a, b or c to complete the text.

My best friend Ian has got many ⁰ _____ . His ¹ _____ names are Nick, Mark, Ruth and Susan. Nick is very ² _____ – I think he's about 190 centimetres. Mark has got short ³ _____ hair. Ruth and Susan ⁴ _____ very pretty. My best friend likes his cousins very much. I like ⁵ _____ too. We often go ⁶ _____ together.

0 a grandparents   (b) relatives   c parents
1 a cousin's   b cousins   c cousins'
2 a tall   b fun   c long
3 a slim   b dark   c shy
4 a have got   b do   c are
5 a their   b them   c theirs
6 a shopping   b a walk   c the cinema   /3

PHOTOCOPIABLE   © Pearson Education Limited 2010

Reading

7 Read the text and tick (✔) true or cross (✗) false.

1 Kate is Anna's aunt. ☐

2 Anna has got three dogs. ☐

3 Maggie sings at family parties. ☐

4 Anna likes listening to The Corrs. ☐

5 Maggie never reads books after school. ☐

6 The three sisters never go to the cinema. ☐

7 Anna sometimes plays tennis on Sunday. ☐

8 Aunt Teresa comes to the girls' house once a week. ☐

/8

home	browse	find	forum	music	video

My name is Anna and I live in Cardiff, the capital city of Wales. I am 16 years old and I have got two young sisters: Kate and Maggie. I have also got two dogs and a cat: the dogs are called Fido and Rex and the cat is called Masha.

Kate loves playing the guitar and Maggie loves singing. She often sings at family parties. I listen to music every day. My favourite pop group is The Corrs. The Corrs are an Irish band. I like their songs very much and I have got all their CDs. I also like Irish folk music. I go to Irish dancing classes on Mondays and Wednesdays.

After school, Maggie often reads her books and Kate usually does her homework. At the weekend, we usually hang out with friends or go to the cinema together. We sometimes watch DVDs.

I have got photos of my family on my mobile phone. I have a nice photo of my favourite relative, my Aunt Teresa. She visits us every Sunday and we sometimes play tennis together. She's very friendly and she's fun!

Do you think we can make friends? If you do, then write to me soon.

Listening

8 ⟨2⟩ Listen and match the speakers with the topics.

1 Alex   **a** work on a computer

2 Frank   **b** drive a car

3 Gina   **c** do sports

4 Martha   **d** eat sandwiches and chocolate at work

/4

9 ⟨2⟩ Listen again and answer the questions.

1 Where do Alex and Jack watch DVDs?

_____

2 What does Frank do after work?

_____

3 What time does Gina have dinner?

_____

4 How many classes does Martha teach every day?

_____

/4

Communication

10 Complete the sentences with a word in each gap.

1 A: _____ old is he?

   B: He's sixteen.

2 That's all _____ now.

   Love, Jane

3 A: _____ , Sarah. I'm Tom.

   B: Hi, Tom. Pleased to _____ you.

4 A: Where are you from _____ Poland?

   B: _____ from Warsaw. You know, it's the capital city.

5 Dear Mum and Dad,

   How are you? I'm _____ .

   I'm _____ in Manchester! It's great!

6 A: What's your brother's _____ ?

   B: It's Jan.

/9

Marks	
Vocabulary and grammar	/25 marks
Reading	/8 marks
Listening	/8 marks
Communication	/9 marks
Total:	/50 marks

Units 1&2   language and skills test 1b

Name: ....

Vocabulary & Grammar

1 Cross out the word that you cannot use with the word in bold.

0 **play** badminton/~~skiing~~/football
1 shoe/music/news **shop**
2 fire/post/police **station**
3 **do** running/karate/judo
4 **go** gymnastics/rowing/swimming

/4

2 Write in the missing letters to complete the words in each category.

Sports: golf, rugby, v _ _ _ _ _ _ _ _
Body: head, arm, l _ _
In town: school, cinema, h _ _ _ _ _ _ _
Shops: stationery shop, bookshop, p _ _ _ _ _ _
Illnesses: a cold, a headache, a s _ _ _ leg
Rooms: hall, bedroom, b _ _ _ _ _ _

/6

3 Replace the underlined adjective in each sentence with the correct one from the words below.

interesting ✔   polluted   brilliant
famous   terrible

0 We've got some pretty museums in my city.   _interesting_
1 The weather here is fantastic. It's cold and it rains all the time.   _____
2 The music at the concert was shy. I loved it!   _____
3 Many people come to London to see the good-looking London Eye.   _____
4 My city is very exciting, but it is also interesting. There is a lot of traffic.   _____

/2

4 Put the words in the correct order to form sentences with *can*.

0 well/Heather/speak/can/quite/English/.
   Heather can speak English quite well.
1 teacher/the/play/can/piano?/your/
   _____
2 well/very/I/cycle/can't/.
   _____
3 badminton/you/play/well?/can/
   _____
4 swim/Lee/well/Mark/and/can/.
   _____

/4

5 Underline the correct word(s) to complete the sentences.

0 I haven't got *much/many* money.
1 *Not touch/Don't touch* the computer! It's mine!
2 Margaret runs very *quickly/quick*.
3 I haven't got *a/any* pet.
4 There aren't *much/many* clothes in my wardrobe.
5 *You open/Open* the window, please. It's very hot in here.
6 Ron's grandmother is a very *happily/happy* person.
7 How *much/many* schools are there in your town?
8 Is there *some/any* water in the fridge?

/4

6 Complete the text with one word in each gap.

I've got a 0 _____lot_____ of friends but Debbie and Sheila are my best friends. They're very good at sport. They 1 _____ basketball three times a week and go rock 2 _____ with Debbie's older brother every summer. Sheila also loves music and she 3 _____ sing quite well. Debbie reads a lot in her free time. She's got 4 _____ books in her bedroom. But there aren't 5 _____ books about history because Debbie doesn't like history.

/5

PHOTOCOPIABLE   © Pearson Education Limited 2010

Reading

7 Read the text about shopping and choose the correct answers.

1 How often do the girls go shopping?
  a once a day   **b** once a week
  c once a month

2 What do they have to drink in the café?
  a tea   **b** coffee   **c** hot chocolate

3 What is 'Denim & Fashion'?
  a a clothes shop   **b** a shoe shop
  c a music shop

4 What do the girls do in Music World?
  a They buy Dido CDs.
  b They watch Marcus Miller DVDs.
  c They listen to music.

5 How often do the girls buy CDs?
  a always   **b** rarely   **c** never

6 When the girls feel hungry, they go to
  a the baker's.   **b** a fast food restaurant.
  c home.

7 The girls like the _____ in the fast food restaurant.
  a food   **b** music   **c** plants

8 What do the girls buy in the baker's?
  a a delicious cake   **b** a chocolate snack
  c a cheese sandwich

/8

Susie, me and shopping

Believe it or not – shopping is my life! I love shopping. Every weekend I go to a shopping mall with my friend Susie and we spend a lot of time there – usually four hours! We always have a cup of hot chocolate in a small café, and sit and relax for an hour or two. Then we go to Denim & Fashion, our favourite clothes shop – it has got great clothes. Unfortunately we never stop at the High Heel shoe shop because the shoes are very expensive and we haven't got much money.

We sometimes go to Music World to look at new CDs or DVDs. I like Dido, an English singer and Susie loves Marcus Miller, a guitarist. We don't often buy any CDs but we like listening to them in the shop. When we are hungry, we go to a fast food restaurant to have a burger and a cola. It's not very healthy but it's a nice place to sit and there are lots of plants in the restaurant. Next to the restaurant, there is a baker's with delicious cakes. We sometimes buy a chocolate snack there. Sometimes we go to the cinema to see a film when we finish shopping. We love hanging out in our shopping mall!

Listening

8 ⓷ Listen to a survey about sports. Tick (✔) true and cross (✗) false.

1 Mike plays in a school football team. ☐
2 Mike has three favourite footballers. ☐
3 Steven is a good surfer. ☐
4 Mick Fanning is from Australia. ☐
5 Jodie goes to the climbing wall three times a week. ☐
6 Jodie uses ropes on a climbing wall. ☐
7 Georgia doesn't think skateboarding is exciting. ☐
8 Georgia hasn't got a skateboarding hero. ☐

/8

Communication

9 Write questions for the answers. Use the prompts in bold.

1 Q: _____ **get**
  Go down High Street and the museum is on your left.

2 Q: _____ **near**
  The Starlight Cinema? Yes, it's two minutes from here.

3 Q: _____ **team**
  Favourite? Yes, I have. It's Manchester United.

4 Q: _____ **or**
  My town? It's big.

5 Q: _____ **any**
  Yes, I do. I play tennis every Friday.

/5

10 Complete the sentences with a word in each gap.

1 Turn right and then _____ the second left into Jackson Road.
2 Let's _____ to my house to watch a DVD.
3 _____ you at the theatre at 7 p.m.
4 Excuse me, can you _____ that again, please?

/4

Marks	
Vocabulary and grammar	/25 marks
Reading	/8 marks
Listening	/8 marks
Communication	/9 marks
Total:	**/50 marks**

Units 3&4   language and skills test 2a

Name: ....

Vocabulary & Grammar

1 Cross out the word that you cannot use with the word in bold.

0 **play** badminton /~~skiing~~/football

1 clothes/green/sports **shop**

2 **have** sick/a headache/a cold

3 **go** karate/swimming/running

4 **do** gymnastics/judo/baseball

/4

2 Write in the missing letters to complete the words in each category.

Extreme sports: skateboarding, surfing, rock c _ _ _ _ _ _ _

Body: neck, shoulder, f _ _ _ _ r

In town: library, hotel, post o _ _ _ _ _

Shops: bookshop, shoe shop, b _ _ _ _ _

Illnesses: a cough, a toothache, a p _ _ _ in the knee

In the kitchen: cupboard, fridge, c _ _ _ _ _

/6

3 Replace the underlined adjective in each sentence with the correct one from the words below.

> interesting ✔   exciting   terrible
> famous   polluted

0 We've got some <u>pretty</u> museums in my city.   *interesting*

1 Many people want to see the <u>friendly</u> Big Ben in London.   _____

2 Come and visit me. There are many <u>tall</u> places in my city.   _____

3 There's a lot of traffic in my town and it's very <u>good-looking</u>.   _____

4 It's cold and rainy all the time here. The weather is <u>great</u>.   _____

/2

4 Put the words in the correct order to form sentences with *can*.

0 well/Heather/speak/can/quite/English/.
Heather can speak English quite well.

1 very/play/he/well/can't/golf/.
_____

2 Ruth/well/Imogen/sing/and/can/.
_____

3 dance/parents/samba?/can/your/the/
_____

4 you/motorbike/a/can/well?/ride/
_____

/4

5 <u>Underline</u> the correct word(s) to complete the sentences.

0 I haven't got <u>much</u>/many money.

1 Tom is a very *well/good* swimmer.

2 There aren't *a /any* swimming pools in my town.

3 *Close/You close* the window, please. It's very cold here.

4 Have you got *some/any* perfume in your bag?

5 I haven't got *many/much* shampoo.

6 *Don't run/Not run* long distances for two months.

7 How *much/many* bathrooms are there in your house?

8 My father drives very *safely/safe*.

/4

6 Complete the text with one word in each gap.

I've got a ⁰ ___*lot*___ of friends but Peter and Chris are my best friends. They're very good at sport. They ¹ _____ swim very well and they're also good at baseball and tennis (they ² _____ tennis at school with our PE teacher). Peter likes surfing – he's very happy now because he's got a new ³ _____ and wetsuit. Chris hasn't got ⁴ _____ sports equipment – only a helmet for cycling. He doesn't need ⁵ _____ sports clothes because he cycles to school in his school uniform.

/5

Reading

7 Read the text about shopping and choose the correct answers.

1 How much time do the girls spend in the shopping mall?

   a two hours **b** three hours **c** four hours

2 Where do they drink chocolate?

   a in a café **b** in a sweet shop

   c in a restaurant

3 High Heel is a

   a music shop. **b** shoe shop.

   c clothes shop.

4 How often do the girls go to Music World?

   a often **b** sometimes **c** never

5 Susie really likes

   a Marcus Miller's music. **b** Dido's songs.

   c nothing.

6 The girls go to a restaurant when they are

   a hungry. **b** tired. **c** happy.

7 What is next to the fast food restaurant?

   a a cinema **b** a snack bar **c** a baker's

8 What do the girls think about shopping in the shopping mall?

   a They enjoy it a lot. **b** They don't like it.

   c They sometimes like it.

/8

> **Susie, me and shopping**
>
> Believe it or not – shopping is my life! I love shopping. Every weekend I go to a shopping mall with my friend Susie and we spend a lot of time there – usually four hours! We always have a cup of hot chocolate in a small café, and sit and relax for an hour or two. Then we go to Denim & Fashion, our favourite clothes shop – it has got great clothes. Unfortunately we never stop at the High Heel shoe shop because the shoes are very expensive and we haven't got much money.
>
> We sometimes go to Music World to look at new CDs or DVDs. I like Dido, an English singer and Susie loves Marcus Miller, a guitarist. We don't often buy any CDs but we like listening to them in the shop. When we are hungry, we go to a fast food restaurant to have a burger and a cola. It's not very healthy but it's a nice place to sit and there are lots of plants in the restaurant. Next to the restaurant, there is a baker's with delicious cakes. We sometimes buy a chocolate snack there. Sometimes we go to the cinema to see a film when we finish shopping. We love hanging out in our shopping mall!

Listening

8 ⟨3⟩ Listen to a survey about sports. Tick (✔) true and cross (✗) false.

1 Mike plays football once a week. ☐

2 Mike thinks Ronaldinho is a good footballer. ☐

3 Steven doesn't like watching surfing. ☐

4 Mike Fanning is from England. ☐

5 Jodie doesn't like climbing a wall. ☐

6 Arlene Blum comes from the USA. ☐

7 Georgia can't do skateboarding. ☐

8 Georgia thinks all skateboarders are heroes. ☐

/8

Communication

9 Write questions for the answers. Use the prompts in bold.

1 Turn left into Market Road.

   Q: _____ **again**

   Sure, no problem. Turn left into Market Road.

2 Q: _____ **how**

   Take the second right into Cross Street. The National Bank is on the right.

3 Q: _____ **can**

   In the evenings, you can watch TV, go to the cinema or theatre, or meet with friends!

4 Q: _____ **TV**

   I usually watch football and tennis.

5 Q: _____ **service**

   The buses are good but there isn't a train service.

/5

10 Complete the sentences with a word in each gap.

1 See you _____ 3 p.m., after school!

2 Come to my house and _____ my family.

3 A: I can't find a map of the city in this shop.

   B: Look! _____ a map of the city.

4 You can't _____ it! It's on your left!

/4

Marks	
Vocabulary and grammar	/25 marks
Reading	/8 marks
Listening	/8 marks
Communication	/9 marks
Total:	**/50 marks**

Units 3&4 language and skills test 2b

Name: ....

Vocabulary & Grammar

1 Write the words below in the correct category. Then add two more words to each group.

> tomatoes   dress   shirt
> username   biscuits   blogs

Food:

_____ , _____ ,

e _ _ _ , o _ _ _ _ _

Clothes:

_____ , _____ ,

s _ _ a _ _ _ , h _ _ _ _ _

The internet:

_____ , _____ ,

web p _ _ _ , d _ _ n _ _ _ _

/9

2 Underline the correct word(s) to complete the sentences.

0 We always have sandwiches for *breakfast/ lunch* at school at 1.30 p.m.

1 Potatoes are my favourite *vegetable/fruit*.

2 Your trousers are too big. You need a *belt/scarf*.

3 First *cut/put* the apples into small pieces.

4 I like *sending/chatting* with my friends online.

/2

3 Correct the mistake in each sentence.

0 ~~I'm cycling~~ to school every day.

   I cycle to school every day.

1 I love play basketball.

_____

2 Maria has breakfast now.

_____

3 What time are you usually getting up?

_____

4 My little sister doesn't like to helping at home.

_____

5 Robert is doing karate three times a week.

_____

6 Listen! The teacher speaks to us.

_____

/6

4 Add an article *a*, *an* or *the*, or nothing (–) to the sentences.

0 I've got ___*a*___ brother and two sisters.

1 You need _____ apple for this recipe.

2 I don't like _____ boys in your class because they're not nice.

3 Becky's parents are doctors and she wants to be _____ doctor too.

4 My brother doesn't drink _____ milk.

5 Can you see a girl dancing with a tall boy? _____ girl is my brother's girlfriend.

/5

5 Choose the best answer a, b or c to complete the text.

My older brother Chris is a vegetarian – he doesn't eat **0** _____ . But he loves **1** _____ food and often eats in Chinese, Japanese and Mexican restaurants. I sometimes **2** _____ with him but not very often. Chris can cook quite well, too. And he loves **3** _____ ! I like his green salad very much. He takes some lettuce and then **4** _____ some lemon juice and oil together and pours it on the lettuce. Today, Chris **5** _____ a cheese pizza for me and my parents. We all love **6** _____ pizza!

0 a snacks   (b) meat   c rice
1 a foreign   b ready   c traditional
2 a am going   b goes   c go
3 a cooks   b cooking   c cook
4 a mixes   b boils   c cuts
5 a 's making   b makes   c making
6 a the   b a   c –

/3

PHOTOCOPIABLE   © Pearson Education Limited 2010

Reading

6 Read the magazine article and match the headings a–d with paragraphs 1–4.

a Online fashion ___

b Online shops meet young people's needs ___

c Why go online shopping? ___

d Online products for young people ___

/4

7 Read the text again and answer the questions.

1 Why is online shopping good?

_____

2 What do young people look at in online music shops?

_____

3 How do the girls want to look at a party?

_____

4 What do online shop owners know about young people's styles?

_____

/4

ONLINE SHOPPING

1 Online shopping is shopping on the internet. This is a great way of shopping for young people nowadays. Why? Because it is fast and easy and because you can buy products in online shops which you cannot buy in a normal shop. Another important thing is that the products in an online shop are usually cheaper.

2 What do young people buy on the internet? Many of them look for music and games. They look at the prices of new CDs and DVDs in online music shops. They look for new types of MP3 players – and good prices! They also try to find new and interesting games to buy and play with friends in their free time.

3 Girls buy clothes over the internet: jeans, dresses, sweaters, skirts, hats and jewellery like earrings and piercings. Some buy old clothes, for example from the 70s and 80s, when they want to look cool at a party. You can find clothes for all kinds of styles: punk, Indie, Goth.

4 Online shop owners know about young people's likes and dislikes. They do their best to sell things they know young people like. They know that young people's styles often change, so they offer a big choice of products. Also their websites are exciting and interesting to look at.

Listening

8 ⓸ Listen to the radio interview and complete the sentences with a word in each gap.

1 Marie is a _____ model.

2 Marie goes to the gym every _____ .

3 She often goes _____ in the morning.

4 Marie's favourite drink is _____ juice.

5 Marie sometimes _____ for her friends.

6 She likes _____ recipes.

7 Marie thinks that soups are _____ .

8 Marie is in London for a _____ competition.

/8

Communication

9 Complete the dialogues with a word in each gap.

1 **A:** Can I help you?

   B: I'd _____ a cheese sandwich.

   A: Here you are.

   B: How _____ is it?

   A: It's £1.50. _____ else?

   B: No, thanks.

2 **A:** What _____ you like to drink?

   B: I'll _____ a hot chocolate.

   A: That's £5, _____ .

3 **A:** Do you _____ to go to the cinema?

   B: That's a good _____ .

4 **A:** I think people in the UK have lunch at 1 o'clock.

   B: I'm not _____ .

/9

Marks	
Vocabulary and grammar	/25 marks
Reading	/8 marks
Listening	/8 marks
Communication	/9 marks
Total:	**/50 marks**

Units 5&6   language and skills test 3a

Name: ....

Vocabulary & Grammar

1 Write the words below in the correct category. Then add two more words to each group.

> meat   chatroom   download
> trousers   cereal   boots

Clothes:

_____ , _____ ,

t _ _ _n _ _ _ , j _ _ k _ _

The internet:

_____ , _____ ,

p _ _ s _ _ _ _ , l _ _ on

Food:

_____ , _____ ,

f _ _ _ , b _ n _ _ _ _

/9

2 Underline the correct word(s) to complete the sentences.

0 We always have sandwiches for *breakfast/ lunch* at school at 1.30 p.m.

1 It's very cold today. Take your *skirt/sweater* with you.

2 First, you need to boil *the potatoes/the crisps*.

3 I often do *blog/research* on the internet.

4 Apples are my favourite *vegetable/fruit*.

/2

3 Correct the mistake in each sentence.

0 ~~I'm cycling~~ to school every day.
   I cycle to school every day.

1 Don't talk so loudly! The baby sleeps.

   _____

2 They don't like to getting up early.

   _____

3 Jane reads a book at the moment.

   _____

4 What are you usually having for lunch?

   _____

5 I hate watch football on TV.

   _____

6 Tim is going skiing twice a year.

   _____

/6

4 Add an article *a*, *an* or *the*, or nothing (–) to the sentences.

0 I've got ___*a*___ brother and two sisters.

1 Can you see a boy talking to two girls? _____ boy is from my school.

2 You need _____ cheese and some tomatoes to make the sandwich.

3 I like _____ girls in your class because they're fun.

4 Tom's parents are teachers and he wants to be _____ teacher too.

5 We've got _____ armchair and two sofas in our living room.

/5

5 Choose the best answer a, b or c to complete the text.

My older sister Olivia ⁰ _____ fashion and she's very stylish. She always ¹ _____ nice clothes and sometimes she wears a big ² _____ on her head. I am different. I hate ³ _____ up in the morning so I get dressed very quickly. Today I ⁴ _____ a white T-shirt and my favourite blue jeans. I hate ⁵ _____ dresses but my sister loves them. We're very different. We like different food, too. My sister loves healthy food and I love ⁶ _____ meals.

0 **a** love	**b** loves	**c** loving
1 **a** wears	**b** 's wearing	**c** wear
2 **a** belt	**b** earring	**c** hat
3 **a** getting	**b** get	**c** to get
4 **a** wear	**b** 'm wearing	**c** wearing
5 **a** the	**b** a	**c** –
6 **a** traditional	**b** ready	**c** foreign

/3

Reading

6 **Read the magazine article and match the headings a–d with paragraphs 1–4.**

a Products young people like ___
b What to wear ___
c A great way to shop ___
d Great websites ___

/4

7 **Read the text again and answer the questions.**

1 Why is online shopping good for young people?

____

2 What do young people look for on the internet?

____

3 Where do the girls want to look cool?

____

4 What do online shop owners know about?

____

/4

ONLINE SHOPPING

1 Online shopping is shopping on the internet. This is a great way of shopping for young people nowadays. Why? Because it is fast and easy and because you can buy products in online shops which you cannot buy in a normal shop. Another important thing is that the products in an online shop are usually cheaper.

2 What do young people buy on the internet? Many of them look for music and games. They look at the prices of new CDs and DVDs in online music shops. They look for new types of MP3 players – and good prices! They also try to find new and interesting games to buy and play with friends in their free time.

3 Girls buy clothes over the internet: jeans, dresses, sweaters, skirts, hats and jewellery like earrings and piercings. Some buy old clothes, for example from the 70s and 80s, when they want to look cool at a party. You can find clothes for all kinds of styles: punk, Indie, Goth.

4 Online shop owners know about young people's likes and dislikes. They do their best to sell things they know young people like. They know that young people's styles often change, so they offer a big choice of products. Also their websites are exciting and interesting to look at.

Listening

8 **(4) Listen to the radio interview and complete the sentences with a word in each gap.**

1 Marie goes for a walk __________ a week.
2 Marie eats vegetables and lots of __________ .
3 Marie doesn't like drinking __________ .
4 Marie often has __________ sandwiches.
5 Marie loves __________ food very much.
6 When she cooks, she uses recipes from __________ .
7 Marie really likes __________ soup.
8 In London, Marie is in a __________ competition.

/8

Communication

9 **Complete the dialogues with a word in each gap.**

1 **A:** Can I have a ______ of carrot cake, please?
B: ______ you are. ______'s £2.50.
A: Thank you.

2 **A:** What would you like to drink?
B: A fruit ______ , please. ______much is it?
A: £1, please.
B: Here's a £5 note.
A: Thank you. And here's your ________ .

3 **A:** Jack, what are you doing?
B: I'm watching a fantastic movie. Come and ______ me!
A: I'm sorry, I ________ . I'm doing my homework now.

4 **A:** I'm sure people in the UK like drinking tea at 3 o'clock.
B: That's right. I ______ with you.

/9

Marks	
Vocabulary and grammar	/25 marks
Reading	/8 marks
Listening	/8 marks
Communication	/9 marks
Total:	**/50 marks**

Name: ....

Vocabulary & Grammar

1 Write in the missing letters to complete the sentences.

0 Can I use your e _lectric_ toothbrush? I need to brush my teeth.

1 I love _ _ _ ss _ _ _ _ music. My favourite is Mozart.

2 My little sister is three today. She's got three _ _ _ d _ _ _ on her birthday cake.

3 Adolph Rickenbacker _ _ v _ _ _ _ d the electric guitar.

4 Can you wake me up tomorrow? My _ _ _ _ m clock doesn't work.

5 I like listening to j _ _ _ . And what kind of music do you like?

6 In your country, do you send _ _ r _ _ to your friends and family at Christmas?

/6

2 Correct the <u>underlined</u> word in each sentence.

0 Rachel needs a <u>toaster</u>. She wants to dry her hair before she goes to school. *hairdryer*

1 We use an electric <u>toothbrush</u> to boil water. _____

2 I often listen to the <u>TV</u> in my car. _____

3 Do you wear special <u>sweets</u> to festivals in your country? _____

4 Who <u>developed</u> and built the Eiffel Tower in Paris? _____

5 Today people can travel <u>convenient</u> to many places. _____

/5

3 Complete the sentences with the past simple form of the verbs below.

> not enjoy   be   have ✔   send
> not go   wake up

0 We ___*had*___ cereal for breakfast yesterday.

1 Where _____ you yesterday at 5 p.m.?

2 I _____ at 10 a.m. on Sunday morning.

3 We _____ to school last week.

4 Tom _____ the party – it was boring!

5 I _____ him an email on Monday.

/5

4 Correct the mistake in each of the sentences.

0 Why did she puts my T-shirt in the washing machine?
   Why did she put my T-shirt in the washing machine?

1 I didn't wore my school uniform yesterday.

_____

2 Who did created Facebook?

_____

3 My father give me £10 two days ago.

_____

4 Who did you went with to the party on Saturday?

_____

5 Why did Hannah unhappy last night?

_____

6 They was very tired yesterday after school.

_____

/6

5 Choose the best word a, b or c to complete the email.

Hi Becky,
I'm sorry I **0** ___*didn't*___ call you from Paris but I didn't have my mobile phone **1** _____ with me! You know me – I often forget things.
The New Year celebrations in Paris **2** _____ great! I especially liked the **3** _____ at midnight. Absolutely fantastic! And very long, too! – about 30 minutes.
And how **4** _____ your Christmas? Did your mother **5** _____ her wonderful cakes? And what presents **6** _____ you get?
Lots of love and hope to hear from you soon,
Heather

0 a don't   (b) didn't   c wasn't
1 a charger   b player   c cooker
2 a did   b were   c was
3 a cards   b fireworks   c presents
4 a was   b did   c were
5 a made   b makes   c make
6 a were   b was   c did

/3

PHOTOCOPIABLE   © Pearson Education Limited 2010

Reading

6 Read the text about the Battle of Hastings. Tick (✔) true or cross (✗).

1 The writer really likes Hastings. ☐
2 There is an old castle in Hastings. ☐
3 The Battle of Hastings didn't change English history. ☐
4 William the Conqueror attacked the Norman army. ☐
5 There were 15,500 people in the battle in 1066. ☐
6 Harold Godwinson was alive after the battle. ☐
7 People wear traditional clothes at the festival. ☐
8 In 2006, 25,000 people watched the 'Battle' of Hastings. ☐

/8

The **Battle of Hastings** today

Last week I went to Hastings in the south of England. It's one of my favourite places in England. It is a beautiful historical town by the sea. There are lovely old houses and also part of an old castle at the top of a green hill.

Hastings is famous for a very important event in British history – the Battle of Hastings. The battle took place on 14 October 1066 and it changed English history. The Norman army with its leader, William the Conqueror, attacked the Anglo-Saxon army. There were 8,000 people in the Norman army and 7,500 Anglo-Saxons. They rode horses and also fought the battle on foot. It was a long and hard battle and almost 8,000 people died. The Anglo-Saxon leader, Harold Godwinson, was killed and William the Conqueror became the leader of England.

Every October, people celebrate the Norman victory with a festival in Hastings. They wear traditional clothes, they ride horses and they act out important moments of the battle. Then they eat traditional food and watch fireworks.

The first Hastings festival took place in 1984. At the festival in 2000, there were 1,000 'actors' on foot and 100 people rode horses. And in 2006, 3,500 people took part in the event and 25,000 people watched it. The festival was amazing!

Listening

7 ⑤ Listen to a conversation about Leonardo da Vinci and answer the questions.

1 How often can you listen to *Meet the Genius*?
_____

2 What university is Vincent Leonard from?
_____

3 Where was da Vinci born? _____
4 Who was Verocchio? _____
5 Which three Italian cities did da Vinci travel to in his life? _____
6 What machines did da Vinci draw?
_____

7 What did the King of France give da Vinci?
_____

8 Where did da Vinci die? _____

/8

Communication

8 Write questions for the answers.

1 I had lunch in a French restaurant.
_____

2 I went with my cousin.
_____

3 Yes, I had a great time.
_____

/3

9 Rearrange the sentences in the correct order to make a dialogue.

a Single or return? ___
b Platform 5, in 30 minutes. ___
c Thanks. Bye. ___
d Single, please. ___
e Can I have two student tickets to Hastings, please? _1_
f Here you are. What platform is the next train? ___
g The tickets are £11 each so that's £22, please. ___

/6

Marks	
Vocabulary and grammar	/25 marks
Reading	/8 marks
Listening	/8 marks
Communication	/9 marks
Total:	**/50 marks**

Units 7&8   language and skills test 4a

Name: ....

Vocabulary & Grammar

1 **Write in the missing letters to complete the sentences.**

0 Can I use your e _l e c t r i c_ toothbrush? I need to brush my teeth.

1 Do you eat s _ _ _ _ _ l food at Christmas in your country?

2 Do you want to listen to this song? Here is my MP3 _ _ _ y _ _ .

3 I like _ i _ - _ _ p. And what's your favourite kind of music?

4 I don't really like _ _ _ _ y metal. I prefer rock and pop music.

5 In my country we usually have New Year's Eve parties with nice music and d _ _ _ i _ _ .

6 Gustave Eiffel _ _ s _ _ _ _ d and built the Eiffel Tower in Paris.

/6

2 **Correct the underlined word in each sentence.**

0 Rachel needs a <u>toaster</u>. She wants to dry her hair before she goes to school. _hairdryer_

1 I often listen to the <u>TV</u> after work. _____

2 Oh, no! My mobile phone isn't working and I forgot my phone <u>cooker</u>. _____

3 Who <u>built</u> antibiotics? _____

4 What films do you watch on the <u>radio</u>? _____

5 I like my <u>electric</u> phone. It's easy to use. _____

/5

3 **Complete the sentences with the past simple form of the verbs below.**

be   give   clean ✔   not go
sell   not have

0 We _cleaned_ our rooms yesterday.

1 They _____ swimming yesterday. The weather was terrible.

2 My aunt _____ me a beautiful handbag for my birthday.

3 I _____ any homework last week.

4 Why _____ Sandra late for school yesterday?

5 Robert's grandparents _____ their house and moved to California.

/5

4 **Correct the mistake in each of the sentences.**

0 Why did she puts my T-shirt in the washing machine?

   Why did she put my T-shirt in the
   washing machine?

1 I wake up many times last night.

   _____

2 Who did you went with to the cinema last night?

   _____

3 I didn't sent him an email yesterday.

   _____

4 Who did made the first mobile phone call?

   _____

5 Where you be last night?

   _____

6 Robert were in London three years ago.

   _____

/6

5 **Choose the best word a, b or c to complete the email.**

How are you? I'm sorry I ⁰ ___didn't___ write to you last week but I ¹ _____ really busy. It was my mum's 40th birthday last Friday. We bought her a big cake with 40 ² _____ on it. She loved it! My sister gave her a very nice ³ _____ because our mum loves drinking tea. I ⁴ _____ buy her a present but I organised a party for her. I think she ⁵ _____ it very much.
And how are you doing? Is everything alright? ⁶ _____ you go to the cinema with Fiona at the weekend?
Hope to see you soon,
Nick

0	a wasn't	(b) didn't	c don't
1	a did	b were	c was
2	a candles	b presents	c cards
3	a toaster	b alarm clock	c electric kettle
4	a wasn't	b didn't	c don't
5	a liked	b likes	c like
6	a Were	b Did	c Was

/3

PHOTOCOPIABLE   © Pearson Education Limited 2010

Reading

6 Read the text about the Battle of Hastings. Tick (✔) true or cross (✗).

1 Hastings is near the sea. ☐

2 There is a castle on a hill in Hastings. ☐

3 The Battle of Hastings took place in November. ☐

4 Harold Godwinson was the Norman leader. ☐

5 The armies didn't use horses. ☐

6 The celebration of the Battle of Hastings takes place every year in October. ☐

7 People eat at the celebrations. ☐

8 In 2000, 1,000 people rode horses in the 'Battle' of Hastings. ☐

/8

The **Battle of Hastings** today

Last week I went to Hastings in the south of England. It's one of my favourite places in England. It is a beautiful historical town by the sea. There are lovely old houses and also part of an old castle at the top of a green hill.

Hastings is famous for a very important event in British history – the Battle of Hastings. The battle took place on 14 October 1066 and it changed English history. The Norman army with its leader, William the Conqueror, attacked the Anglo-Saxon army. There were 8,000 people in the Norman army and 7,500 Anglo-Saxons. They rode horses and also fought the battle on foot. It was a long and hard battle and almost 8,000 people died. The Anglo-Saxon leader, Harold Godwinson, was killed and William the Conqueror became the leader of England.

Every October, people celebrate the Norman victory with a festival in Hastings. They wear traditional clothes, they ride horses and they act out important moments of the battle. Then they eat traditional food and watch fireworks.

The first Hastings festival took place in 1984. At the festival in 2000, there were 1,000 'actors' on foot and 100 people rode horses. And in 2006, 3,500 people took part in the event and 25,000 people watched it. The festival was amazing!

Listening

7 ⑤ Listen to a conversation about Leonardo da Vinci and answer the questions.

1 Who is Vincent Leonard? _____

2 When was da Vinci born? _____

3 Who was Verocchio? _____

4 What country did da Vinci travel around? _____

5 Why did he change his drawings of machines? _____

6 Who gave da Vinci a house in France? _____

7 Where did da Vinci die? _____

8 How old was da Vinci when he died? _____

/8

Communication

8 Write questions for the answers.

1 I went to the Science Museum in London.

_____

2 I looked at the cars.

_____

3 I went by train and I walked.

_____

/3

9 Rearrange the sentences in the correct order to make a dialogue.

a Thanks. What time does the film start? ___

b Okay, here are your tickets. Enjoy the film. ___

c Three – that's £12.45, please. ___

d At 5.50, 7.30 and 9 p.m. Which one would you like? ___

e The 7.30 one. ___

f Thanks. Bye. ___

g Can I have three tickets to *The Lord of the Rings*, please? _1_

/6

Marks

Vocabulary and grammar	/25 marks
Reading	/8 marks
Listening	/8 marks
Communication	/9 marks
Total:	**/50 marks**

Units 7&8

language and skills test 4b

Name: ....

Vocabulary & Grammar

1   **Cross out the word that you cannot use with the word(s) in bold.**

0   solar/~~polluted~~/wind **power**

1   cloudy/hot/snow **weather**

2   beach/campsite/adventure **holiday**

3   **travel by** train/foot/pedal boat

4   **recycle** environment/bottles/paper   /4

2   <u>Underline</u> **the correct word(s) to complete the sentences.**

0   *Global/Solar* warming is an important problem.

1   We stayed in a holiday *beach/apartment*.

2   He went there *by/on* mountain bike.

3   There's a lot of rain here – we have a lot of *floods/droughts*.

4   The weather was really *wind/windy* yesterday.   /2

3   **Write in the missing letters to complete the sentences.**

0   We need to create more traffic-free z *o n e s* in our city.

1   Boxes and bottles are examples of p _ _ k _ _ _ _ _ .

2   I can't see much – it's very f _ _ _ _ today.

3   Do you recycle old b _ _ t _ _ _ _ _ and plastic containers?

4   I'm afraid there are not enough green s _ _ _ _ _ in my city.   /4

4   **Put the adjectives into the correct form to complete the sentences.**

0   Your hair's ____*shorter*____ (short) than mine.

1   I think Robert's sister is _____ (beautiful) girl in our school.

2   I'm _____ (good) at Maths than English.

3   My ticket was _____ (cheap) than yours.

4   Which is _____ (messy) room in your house?

5   The book was _____ (interesting) than the film.   /5

5   **Complete the sentences with *going to* and the verbs below.**

> travel   not learn ✔   not wear
> be   go

0   We _*aren't going to learn*_ Chinese – it's too difficult.

1   In the future Sandra _____ a teacher.

2   (you) _____ shopping tomorrow?

3   Next year Mark and Ruth _____ around the world.

4   I _____ this sweater – I don't like it.   /4

6   **Correct the mistake in three of the sentences.**

0   I think the price of cars will to go up next year.

1   Will it cold tomorrow?

2   In the future, everybody will have a mobile.

3   I don't think I'll be here in September.

4   I think Sarah not be at school tomorrow.

5   I think the weather be good tomorrow.

Sentence number	Correct sentence
0	*I think the price of cars will go up next year.*
____	_____
____	_____
____	_____

   /3

7   <u>Underline</u> **the correct word(s) to complete the text.**

I had a fantastic holiday last year. We went ⁰ *by/on* car to France and we stayed in a nice ¹ *hotel/camping*. The weather was good – it was ² *sunny/misty* most of the time, so we went to the beach every day. We also visited two museums and other interesting places because my parents love ³ *walking/sightseeing*. Holidays in France are ⁴ *more expensive/the most expensive* than in my country but we ⁵ *are/will* going to go there next year too. I think I ⁶ *will/won't* learn French at school this term because I want to speak French on holiday next year.   /3

   PHOTOCOPIABLE

Reading

8 Read the messages and complete the sentences with a word in each gap.

1 Anna's friends don't go to school by _____ .

2 Anna's home is close to her _____ .

3 Jean56's mum cares about the environment and also about the _____ she pays for electricity.

4 Claire tries to buy things with less _____ .

/4

9 Read again and answer the questions.

1 How does Anna go to school? _____

2 What do Anna's family do with the rubbish?

_____

3 What do Jean56's family use to save energy?

_____

4 What doesn't Claire use when shopping?

_____

/4

What do you do to care about the environment? Share your ideas with us.

Anna: I think it is very important to care about the place you live in. So what do I do to protect the environment? First of all, I ride a bike to school. It's not very far from home but my friends don't walk or cycle, they often take a bus to school. In my family, we always recycle rubbish. We put all the paper, bottles, plastic and tins in different bins. It's not difficult and it helps save our planet!

Jean56: I agree with Anna. You can do small things to help the environment. At home we use low-energy light bulbs and we always turn off the taps in the kitchen or bathroom. My mum gets angry when we don't turn off the light when we leave a room. She wants to protect the environment but she also doesn't want to pay a lot of money for electricity. And she's absolutely right.

Claire: I try to live a healthy life. I don't eat fast food – it's bad for my health. I never use plastic bags when I go shopping. I choose products with little or no packaging. I don't buy packaged food. My friend says it's more convenient but it's more expensive! I think it's important for everyone to know what they can do to be 'green' and protect the environment.

Listening

10 ⑥ Listen to the conversation and choose the correct answer.

1 Nick came back from New Zealand _____ days ago.

  a two   **b** three   **c** four

2 Nick travelled to New Zealand by

  a car.   **b** plane.   **c** ship.

3 There are two main _____ in New Zealand.

  a rivers   **b** lakes   **c** islands

4 What type of holiday did Nick have in New Zealand?

  a camping   **b** walking   **c** climbing

5 Nick didn't use _____ to travel in New Zealand.

  a a mountain bike   **b** a kayak

  c a car

6 The worst moment for Nick was when he _____ .

  a went climbing.   **b** went kayaking.

  c arrived at a campsite at night.

7 How many rainy days were there?

  a one   **b** three   **c** five

8 Nick is going to go to New Zealand again

  a in two years. **b** next year.   **c** in three years.

/8

Communication

11 Complete the dialogue with the words below.

> over   try   bigger   take   different
> for   like   better   what

A: Can I help you?

B: Yes, please. I'm looking ¹_____ wellies.

A: The wellies are ²_____ there.

B: These ones are nice but I don't really ³_____ the colour. Have you got them in a ⁴_____ colour?

A: How about red?

B: Yes, these are fine. Can I ⁵_____ them on?

A: Of course. ⁶_____ size are you?

B: I'm size 6.

(a moment later)

B: They're a bit small. Have you got a ⁷_____ size?

A: Here, try size 7. Is that size ⁸_____?

B: Yes, they are great, thanks. I'll ⁹_____ these.

/9

Marks	
Vocabulary and grammar	/25 marks
Reading	/8 marks
Listening	/8 marks
Communication	/9 marks
Total:	**/50 marks**

language and skills test 5a   Units 9&10

Name: ....

Vocabulary & Grammar

1 **Cross out the word that you cannot use with the word in bold.**

0 solar/~~polluted~~/wind **power**

1 sightseeing/walking/campsite **holiday**

2 wind/cold/stormy **weather**

3 **recycle** packaging/pollution/bottles

4 **travel** by inline skates/helicopter/motorbike

/4

2 **Underline the correct word(s) to complete the sentences.**

0 *Global*/*Solar* warming is an important problem.

1 They travelled by pedal *boat/ship*.

2 My best friend always goes to school *on/by* foot.

3 We have a lot of *floods/droughts* because there's not much rain in our country.

4 Ruth's father likes travelling *on/by* train.

/2

3 **Write in the missing letters to complete the sentences.**

0 We need to create more traffic-free z *o n e s* in our city.

1 In my family, we always recycle our r _ _ _ _ _ h.

2 Going by bike is very easy here because there are many cycle l _ _ _ _ in my city.

3 I don't want to travel by k _ _ _ _ because I don't like water.

4 We stayed in a holiday _ p _ _ _ _ _ _ t by the beach.

/4

4 **Put the adjectives into the correct form to complete the sentences.**

0 Your hair's ___*shorter*___ (short) than mine.

1 Is your bedroom _____ (big) than your brother's?

2 My questions were _____ (difficult) than hers.

3 My Maths teacher's _____ (intelligent) person I know.

4 I think Cristiano Ronaldo is _____ (great) football player in the world.

5 I'm _____ (good) at Maths than you.

/5

5 **Complete the sentences with *going to* and the verbs below.**

| not learn ✔ | play | wear |
| not join | be | |

0 We __*aren't going to learn*__ Chinese – it's too difficult

1 (you) _____ your new dress tonight?

2 I _____ a doctor in the future.

3 Henry _____ our band – he can't play the guitar.

4 They _____ football tomorrow after school.

/4

6 **Correct the mistake in three of the sentences.**

0 I think the price of cars will to go up next year.

1 I don't think Beth will come to your party.

2 What will the weather like tomorrow?

3 My father won't to be home at Christmas.

4 In the future, more people will use the internet for work.

5 I go university in the future.

Sentence number	Correct sentence
_0_	*I think the price of cars will go up next year.*
_____	_____
_____	_____
_____	_____

/3

7 **Underline the correct word(s) to complete the text.**

I had a terrible holiday last year. We went **0** *by/on* car to France and we stayed in a very expensive bed and **1** *food/breakfast* hotel. The weather was terrible. It was rainy or **2** *stormy/sunny* most of the time, so we didn't go to the beach very often. We came back home after two weeks and the weather in England was **3** *better/the best* than in France. We **4** *aren't/won't* going to go there again next year. I like the sun and I want to go on a **5** *beach/adventure* holiday. Five days in the sun will be great! I think next year we **6** *will/won't* go somewhere hot.

/3

PHOTOCOPIABLE   © Pearson Education Limited 2010

Reading

8 Read the messages and complete the sentences with a word in each gap.

1 Anna _____ to school.
2 Jean56's mother wants the family to _____ off the lights when they leave a room.
3 Claire never buys _____ food.
4 Claire wants people to care about the _____ .

/4

9 Read again and answer the questions.

1 How do Anna's friends go to school?
_____
2 What does Anna's family do with the rubbish?
_____
3 What do Jean56's family always do in the kitchen or bathroom? _____
4 What doesn't Claire eat? _____

/4

Listening

10 ⑥ Listen to the conversation and choose the correct answer.

1 Two days ago, Nick came back from
   a Singapore.   **b** Thailand.   **c** New Zealand.
2 The trip took _____ hours.
   a ten   **b** twelve   **c** fourteen
3 There are _____ main islands in New Zealand.
   a two   **b** three   **c** four
4 Nick went on a _____ holiday.
   a sightseeing **b** walking   **c** camping
5 It was _____ when Nick went kayaking.
   a early morning   **b** in the afternoon
   c late in the evening
6 Whose kayak did water go in?
   a Nick's sister's.   **b** Nick's.   **c** Nobody's.
7 There were three _____ days.
   a rainy   **b** foggy   **c** sunny
8 Nick is going to New Zealand next
   a spring.   **b** winter.   **c** summer.

/8

Marks	
Vocabulary and grammar	/25 marks
Reading	/8 marks
Listening	/8 marks
Communication	/9 marks
Total:	**/50 marks**

What do you do to care about the environment? Share your ideas with us.

Anna: I think it is very important to care about the place you live in. So what do I do to protect the environment? First of all, I ride a bike to school. It's not very far from home but my friends don't walk or cycle, they often take a bus to school. In my family, we always recycle rubbish. We put all the paper, bottles, plastic and tins in different bins. It's not difficult and it helps save our planet!

Jean56: I agree with Anna. You can do small things to help the environment. At home we use low-energy light bulbs and we always turn off the taps in the kitchen or bathroom. My mum gets angry when we don't turn off the light when we leave a room. She wants to protect the environment but she also doesn't want to pay a lot of money for electricity. And she's absolutely right.

Claire: I try to live a healthy life. I don't eat fast food – it's bad for my health. I never use plastic bags when I go shopping. I choose products with little or no packaging. I don't buy packaged food. My friend says it's more convenient but it's more expensive! I think it's important for everyone to know what they can do to be 'green' and protect the environment.

Communication

11 Complete the dialogue with the words below.

> list   looking   there   on   sorry   smaller
> need   take   better

A: Okay, let's look at the ¹_____ . You ²_____ a new jumper.
B: A jumper? Why? It's almost spring.
A: But it's often cold here in spring.

(inside a shop)

C: Good morning, can I help you?
A: Yes, please. I am ³_____ for a jumper.
C: The jumpers are over ⁴_____ .
A: Thanks. I like the brown one. Can I try it ⁵_____?
C: Yes, sure.
A: Oh, I'm ⁶_____ but this jumper is a bit big. Have you got it in a ⁷_____ size?
C: What size are you?
A: I'm S size.
C: Here it is. Try this size. Is it ⁸_____?
A: Yes, it's great. How much is it?
C: £35.
A: I'll ⁹_____ it then. Thanks.

/9

Units 9&10   language and skills test 5b

Name: ....

Vocabulary & Grammar

1 Write the words/expressions below in the correct category. Then add two more words to each group.

> make a speech   teacher   happy
> surprised   photographer
> government

Jobs:

_____ , _____ ,

office w _ _ _ _ _ , p _ _ _ _ _ officer

Feelings:

_____ , _____ ,

b _ _ _ _ , t _ _ _ _

Politics:

_____ , _____ ,

vote in e _ _ _ _ _ _ _ _ , knife c _ _ _ _

/9

2 Cross out the word(s) that you cannot use with the word(s) in bold.

0 talk/~~take~~/write **about your family**
1 offer/bow/receive **a gift**
2 **have** a good memory/patient/good computer skills
3 **work** with children/after people/at night

/3

3 Complete the sentences with *at, in* or *on*.

0 I sent an email to him _on_ Tuesday.
1 My parents met _____ May 1988.
2 Dave usually goes out with his friends _____ Friday night.
3 I was born _____ 13 August.
4 We're quite good _____ playing tennis.
5 We went to the cinema _____ 5 o'clock.
6 What did you do yesterday _____ the evening?

/3

4 Correct the mistake in each sentence.

0 Have you ever rode a horse?
   Have you ever ridden a horse?
1 We haven't find any interesting books in the school library.

_____

2 I've ever driven a car because I'm only 15.

_____

3 Have Eddie ever argued with his grandmother?

_____

4 They has never flown a plane.

_____

/4

5 Underline the correct word(s) to complete the sentences.

0 Robert *have/has* to go to school today.
1 If you aren't hungry, *don't/not* eat the potatoes.
2 *Have you/Do you have* to write this essay for tomorrow?
3 I *have /don't have* to make the sandwiches for school. My mum always does it.
4 If you have a toothache, *go/don't go* to the dentist.

/2

6 Complete the email with one word in each gap.

Hi Helen,
I've got very good news – I've got a new
0 ___job___ ! Last week I started working
in an office and I absolutely love it! I work
with very nice people and we do lots of
things together. My boss has a very good
1 _____ of humour and we have a lot
of fun. The only problem is that I
2 _____ to wear a uniform. I hate it!
And I sometimes work 3 _____ the
weekend.
I hope you're doing fine.
Love,
Becky
P.S. 4 _____ call me on my mobile –
I've lost it!

/4

Reading

7 Read the text about Amsterdam and choose the correct answers.

1 Eddy has been a student for _____ years.
  a two   **b** three   **c** four

2 In Amsterdam, Jonathan stayed
  a at the wooden house.   **b** in a hotel.
  c at Eddy's place.

3 Jonathan visited two _____ in Amsterdam.
  a museums   **b** canals   **c** friendly people

4 Eddy took Jonathan to
  a a flower garden.   **b** an amusement park.
  c the city centre.

/4

8 Read the text again and answer the questions.

1 How did Jonathan travel to Amsterdam?
_____

2 What did Jonathan see in Begijnhof?
_____

3 Why do people in Amsterdam travel to work by bike? _____

4 What is Efteling? _____

/4

> **M**y friend, Jonathan, has recently visited the Netherlands. His older brother, Eddy, is a law student in Amsterdam. He has lived there for four years but Jonathan has never had a chance to visit him. Last month he finally decided to go to Amsterdam. He bought a plane ticket and reserved a room in a hotel near Eddy's apartment for a week.
>
> On the first day, Eddy took his brother on a sightseeing tour around Amsterdam. Jonathan was really happy. He loved the clean city with its beautiful old buildings, historic canals and very friendly people. He visited the famous Rijksmuseum to see the Dutch paintings by Rembrandt. He also went to the Van Gogh Museum. He liked the wooden house in Begijnhof, a very old house from 1470. It is probably the oldest wooden house in the Netherlands.
>
> Jonathan was surprised at the public transport in Amsterdam. It was very well organised. Because it was expensive to park in the city centre, many people travelled to work on their bikes. To see more of the city Jonathan used his brother's bike and found it was a quick and convenient means of transport.
>
> On the last day Eddy took Jonathan to Efteling, a large theme park similar to Disney World in Florida. They spent eight hours having fun on the different rides and relaxing in cafés.

Listening

9 ⑦ Listen to four interviews and match the people 1–4 with activities a–h.

1	Marco	**a**	wants to work for the police.
2	Jasmin	**b**	has got five pets at home.
3	Peter	**c**	is creative.
4	Sheila	**d**	wants to teach Maths.
		e	likes fashion.
		f	has clear goals.
		g	likes holidays.
		h	wants to do a voluntary job in the summer.

/8

Communication

10 Write questions for the answers.

1 Q: _____
_____
I'm from Budapest.

2 Q: _____
_____
I'm patient and polite. I also have good computer skills.

3 Q: _____
_____
I speak German, Spanish and a bit of Russian.

4 Q: _____
_____
I like Maths, of course, and Geography.

/4

11 Complete the sentences with one word.

1 Dear _____ or Madam, …

2 I'm writing to _____ for the post of sales assistant.

3 _____ sincerely, Edna Bright.

4 I can _____ at night.

5 I have good people _____ .

/5

Marks

Vocabulary and grammar	/25 marks
Reading	/8 marks
Listening	/8 marks
Communication	/9 marks
Total:	**/50 marks**

Units 11&12   language and skills test 6a

Name: ....

Vocabulary & Grammar

1 Write the words/expressions below in the correct category. Then add two more words to each group.

> nervous   politicians   hairdresser
> parliament   upset   nurse

Feelings:

_____ , _____ ,

w _ _ r _ _ _ , a _ _ r _

Politics:

_____ , _____ ,

make a s _ _ _ _ _ , v _ _ _ _

Jobs:

_____ , _____ ,

bus d _ _ _ _ _ , shop a _ _ _ _ _ _ _

/9

2 Cross out the word(s) that you cannot use with the word(s) in bold.

0 talk/~~take~~/write **about your family**

1 **to be good at** Maths/playing the guitar/ people

2 greet/receive/offer **a gift**

3 **work** at the weekend/after children/with animals

/3

3 Complete the sentences with *at*, *in* or *on*.

0 I sent an email to him _on_ Tuesday.

1 I'm very bad _____ remembering new words.

2 Sam usually watches gymnastics _____ the TV.

3 Do you always have breakfast _____ the morning?

4 I have a driving test _____ 17 February.

5 We're learning about Africa _____ school now.

6 Mark and John start school _____ the same time.

/3

4 Correct the mistake in each sentence.

0 Have you ever rode a horse?

Have you ever ridden a horse?

1 I want to go to Paris next year because I've ever been there.

_____

2 Have your brother ever helped you with your French homework?

_____

3 We have never spoke about it.

_____

4 My parents haven't meet my History teacher.

_____

/4

5 Underline the correct word(s) to complete the sentences.

0 Robert *have/has* to go to school today.

1 Peter *has to/doesn't have to* hurry. It's 7 a.m. and school starts at 10 a.m. today.

2 If you are tired, *don't/not* go to bed so late.

3 *Do you have to/Have you* wear a uniform to school?

4 If you have a cold, *stay/don't stay* at home tonight.

/2

6 Complete the email with one word in each gap.

Hi Henry,

I've got very good news – I've got a new
0 ___job___ ! Last week I started working
as a photographer. Every day I ¹ _____
photos of many different objects and people.
And I love it! Another good thing is that I
don't ² _____ to wear formal clothes.
I just put on a T-shirt, jeans and my old
trainers. It's great, isn't it?

The only problem is that I work very long
hours. I start at 9 a.m. and often finish at 10
p.m., so I'm usually very ³ _____ .

And how are things with you? Everything
okay?

⁴ _____ forget to say hello to Alicia
from me.

Love, Tom

/4

Reading

7 Read the text about Amsterdam and choose the correct answers.

1 Jonathan's brother studies
  a art.   **b** law.   **c** architecture.

2 Jonathan spent _____ in Amsterdam.
  a seven days   **b** two weeks   **c** a weekend

3 The old house in Begijnhof was over _____ years old.
  a 200   **b** 400   **c** 500

4 In Amsterdam, Jonathan travelled by
  a bus.   **b** car.   **c** bike.

/4

8 Read the text again and answer the questions.

1 What did Jonathan see in the Rijksmuseum?

_____

2 How does the writer describe public transport in Amsterdam? _____

_____

3 When was the wooden house built?

_____

4 What did they do at the theme park?

_____

/4

My friend, Jonathan, has recently visited the Nehterlands. His older brother, Eddy, is a law student in Amsterdam. He has lived there for four years but Jonathan has never had a chance to visit him. Last month he finally decided to go to Amsterdam. He bought a plane ticket and reserved a room in a hotel near Eddy's apartment for a week.

On the first day, Eddy took his brother on a sightseeing tour around Amsterdam. Jonathan was really happy. He loved the clean city with its beautiful old buildings, historic canals and very friendly people. He visited the famous Rijksmuseum to see the Dutch paintings by Rembrandt. He also went to the Van Gogh Museum. He liked the wooden house in Begijnhof, a very old house from 1470. It is probably the oldest wooden house in the Netherlands.

Jonathan was surprised at the public transport in Amsterdam. It was very well organised. Because it was expensive to park in the city centre, many people travelled to work on their bikes. To see more of the city Jonathan used his brother's bike and found it was a quick and convenient means of transport.

On the last day Eddy took Jonathan to Efteling, a large theme park similar to Disney World in Florida. They spent eight hours having fun on the different rides and relaxing in cafés.

Listening

9 ⑦ Listen to four interviews and match the people 1–4 with activities a–h.

1 Marco   **a** wants to work with animals.
2 Jasmin   **b** likes trying out new hairstyles.
3 Peter   **c** knows the job he wants to do is not easy.
4 Sheila   **d** has clear goals.
          e thinks it's important to be reliable.
          f likes watching a vet at work.
          g thinks he is organised and caring
          h thinks it's important to be fit.

/8

Communication

10 Write questions for the answers.

1 Q: _____

_____

I want the job because I need some money for a summer language course in the UK.

2 Q: _____

_____

I speak French, Portuguese and a bit of German.

3 Q: _____

_____

I have good people skills.

4 Q: _____

_____

Yes, just one: do I have to work at the weekend?

/4

11 Complete the sentences with one word.

1 You can _____ me by email or mobile phone.

2 _____ faithfully, John Brown.

3 I look _____ to hearing from you.

4 I have a good _____ of humour.

5 My English is fluent and I also _____ some French.

/5

Marks	
Vocabulary and grammar	/25 marks
Reading	/8 marks
Listening	/8 marks
Communication	/9 marks
Total:	**/50 marks**

Language and skills test 6b   Units 11&12

roleplays

Unit 1

Tell your partner about your best friend. Include the following points:

- your best friend's name and age
- describe him/her
- his/her family and where they are from
- his/her favourite band/pet/sports team

Unit 2

Talk to your English friend about your school day. Include the following points:

- what you do in the morning
- your favourite school subjects
- what time you have lunch and dinner
- how you usually spend your free time

Unit 3

You are visiting Oxford. Ask a person in the street for directions to the cinema. Include the following points:

- ask him/her if the cinema is near
- ask him/her how to get to the cinema
- ask him/her to repeat the directions
- thank him/her for his/her help

Unit 4

Talk to your English friend about sports. Include the following points:

- sports you do
- your favourite sports personality
- sports you watch on TV
- sports you don't like

Unit 5

You are visiting a town in the UK. You are hungry. Go to a fast food restaurant and:

- order something to eat
- say what you want to drink
- ask for the price
- pay and thank the server for the change

Unit 6

You are talking to your English cousin about e-time. Tell him/her what you do on the internet. Include the following points:

- what you buy on the internet
- who you chat to when you use instant messaging
- when you do research for school projects
- games you like playing on the internet

Unit 7

You are at the station in London buying a train ticket. Talk to the ticket clerk and:

- ask for a return ticket to Brighton
- ask about the ticket price and a student reduction
- ask about the time the train leaves
- ask about the platform the train leaves from

Unit 8

Talk to your English friend about a day out in your favourite city. Include the following points:

- where you went
- who you went there with
- how you got there
- what you did there and if you enjoyed it

Unit 9

You are shopping in Cambridge in a clothes shop. Talk to the shop assistant and:

- say what you are looking for
- say what size you are and ask to try it on
- say it is too big/small and ask for a smaller/bigger size
- ask about the price and decide to buy the item

Unit 10

You want to spend Friday evening with your English friend:

- ask about your friend's plans for Friday evening
- suggest what you want to do
- invite your friend to join you
- suggest the time and place of your meeting

Unit 11

You are having an interview for a job as a shop assistant in a sports/clothes/music shop in London. Talk to the shop manager. Include the following points:

- why you want this job
- if you have any sales experience
- what skills and qualities you have got
- ask one of your own questions

Unit 12

Talk to your English friend about your country and:

- say how to greet people you know well/people you do not know well
- what to do when you visit a family home
- where you can eat traditional food in your country
- important political problems for teenagers

Teacher's prompts

Unit 1
- What's your best friend's name?
- How old/tall is s/he?
- What colour is his/her hair?
- Has s/he got any brothers or sisters/cousins?
- What's his/her favourite thing/pet/football team?

Unit 2
- What do you do in the morning?
- What are your favourite school subjects?
- What time do you have lunch and dinner?
- How do you usually spend your free time?

Unit 3
- Yes, it's near here.
- Turn left/right into Cross Street.
- Go straight on.
- Take the second/third left (into River Street).
- (It/The cinema)'s on the right.
- No problem.

Unit 4
- What are your favourite sports?
- What sports do you do?
- Have you got a favourite sports personality?
- What sports do you watch on TV?
- What sports don't you like?

Unit 5
- Can I help you?/What would you like?
- Anything else?
- That's £13.30, please.
- Here you are.
- Here's your change.

Unit 6
- What do you use the internet for?
- What do you buy on the internet?
- Who do you chat to when you use instant messaging?
- When do you do research for school projects?
- What games do you like playing on the internet?

Unit 7
- Can I help you?
- Single or return?
- It's £15.
- The train leaves at 3 p.m./in 15 minutes.
- (The train to Brighton leaves from) Platform 3.

Unit 8
- Where did you go?
- Who did you go with?
- How did you get there?
- What did you do there?

Unit 9
- Can I help you?
- What size are you?
- Here you are.
- Yes, no problem.
- Is this size better?
- It's (£35).

Unit 10
- I'm going to watch something on TV.
- And what are you going to do?
- Okay, thanks. That's a great idea.
- See you on Friday evening.

Unit 11
- Why do you want this job?
- Have you got any sales experience?
- What skills/qualities have you got?
- What languages do you speak?
- Have you got any questions?

Unit 12
- What do you do when you greet people you know/do not know well?
- What do you do when you visit a family home?
- Where can you eat traditional food?
- What are the important political problems for teenagers in your country?

writing tasks

Unit 1

You are a student at an English language school in London. Write an email to your English aunt and:

- ask how she is
- say where you are
- describe your teacher
- describe your friends

Unit 3

You want to spend Saturday evening with your English friend. Write a note to him/her and:

- say what you want to do
- ask your friend to go with you
- suggest a place to meet
- suggest a time to meet

Unit 5

You are on holiday in your favourite town. Write a postcard to your English friend and:

- say where you are
- say who you are with
- describe the town
- describe your favourite shop/café/museum

Unit 7

You stayed at your friend's house for two days. Write an informal letter to your English cousin about what you did. Include the following points:

- greet your cousin and ask how he/she is
- describe what you did on the first day
- describe what you did on the second day
- describe a nice activity you did together

Unit 9

Yesterday you lost something at your English summer school. Write a notice for the school notice board. Include:

- what you lost
- what it looked like
- where you lost it
- your contact details

Unit 11

Write a letter applying for a summer job in a restaurant in London. Include the following points:

- write where you heard about the job
- why you want the job
- describe your skills and abilities
- write how to contact you

photo description tasks

Teacher's prompts

Unit 1–6a

- How often do you go shopping in a shopping mall?
- What do you buy most often?
- Do you buy things on the internet? Why? Why not?

Unit 1–6b

- What is the boy good at? What are his skills and abilities?
- How do you spend your free time?
- Do you use a computer? What for?

Unit 7–12a

- What do you think people enjoy most on this kind of holiday?
- Have you ever gone on a camping holiday? When? Where?
- Where are you going to go this summer? Why?

Unit 7–12b

- What kind of celebrations do you like best?
- How often do you take part in different celebrations?
- Have you ever organised a celebration? What was it? Why?

Unit 1–6a

Describe the photo. Include answers to the following questions:

- Do the girls enjoy shopping? Why do you think so?
- Why are the girls shopping together?

Unit 1–6b

Describe the photo. Include answers to the following questions:

- Do you think this boy likes his room? Why/Why not?
- What does he do in his free time?

Unit 7–12a

Describe the photo. Include the following points:

- type of holiday
- places to stay on this kind of holiday
- what you can do on this kind of holiday
- how expensive and interesting this kind of holiday is

Unit 7–12b

Describe the photo. Include answers to the following questions:

- Are the people enjoying themselves? Why do you think so?
- How do you think they celebrate other important events?

photo description tasks

Name: ....

Vocabulary & Grammar

1 Choose the name for each category from the words below.

> shops   food   health   home
> sport   family✓ clothes

0 sister, husband, grandmother,   _family_
1 swimming, tennis, gymnastics   _____
2 sore throat, cough, headache   _____
3 shoe shop, newsagent's, pharmacy   _____
4 meat, biscuits, tomatoes   _____
5 scarf, hoodie, sweater   _____
6 bathroom, kitchen, living room   _____

/6

2 Correct the underlined verb in each sentence.

0 Do you <u>watch</u> books in your free time? _read_
1 How often do you <u>get</u> for a walk with your dog? _____
2 I'm not well today. I <u>have</u> sick. _____
3 Robert and Tom <u>play</u> judo twice a week.
_____
4 First, boil the eggs and then <u>put</u> them into small pieces. _____
5 I can't <u>chat</u> on because I can't remember my password. _____
6 We usually <u>do</u> lunch at 1.30 p.m. _____
7 They always <u>do</u> skiing in winter. _____

/7

3 Choose the best word a, b or c to complete the sentences.

0 Gill's got ____ fair hair.
  (a)long   b dark   c tall
1 I've got a packet of ____ in my bag.
  a sunglasses   b tissues   c earphones
2 I like sitting on the ____ after dinner and reading a book.
  a sofa   b bookcase   c cupboard
3 The weather is ____ here, it's cold and it rains all the time.
  a polluted   b terrible   c great
4 People have got five fingers and five ____ .
  a elbows   b arms   c toes
5 You need a rope for ____ .
  a rowing   b skateboarding   c rock climbing

6 She's very ____ because she doesn't eat much and she does a lot of sport.
  a slim   b pretty   c shy

/3

4 Complete the sentences with the correct form of the verbs below.

> play   create   visit   go✓
> not drink   go   not walk

0 Kirk _goes_ swimming on Sundays.
1 Can you _____ web pages?
2 My girlfriend _____ apple juice. She hates it!
3 They _____ football with their friends at the moment.
4 Please, _____ fast! I've got a pain in my knee.
5 Francis loves _____ to the cinema.
6 We always _____ our relatives in the summer.

/6

5 Underline the correct word(s) to complete the sentences.

0 Can your sister _dance/dances_?
1 Robert can speak English very _good/well_.
2 This is _my/mine_ MP3 player, not yours!
3 My best _friend's/friends'_ name is Derek.
4 Tell _them/their_ about the Maths test on Tuesday.
5 How _much/many_ books have you got?
6 There are 300 _child/children_ in his school.

/3

6 Correct the mistake in each sentence.

0 Ruth never eats ~~the~~ cereal, she hates it!
  Ruth never eats cereal, she hates it!
1 I get up at 7 o'clock always.
  _____
2 My mother's the teacher.
  _____
3 Is Tom like playing badminton?
  _____
4 How many sisters have Patricia got?
  _____
5 There isn't a milk in the fridge.
  _____

/5

Reading

7 Read the text about couch potatoes and choose the correct answers.

1 People who have a healthy life
  a are usually doing something.
  b don't have much sleep.
  c never rest after work.

2 Some people are couch potatoes because
  a they don't like going to school or work.
  b they don't do anything in their free time.
  c they love watching DVDs.

3 A 'couch potato' can be
  a a child.   b an adult.   c a child or adult.

4 A 'couch potato' often _____ the same video game.
  a does   b plays   c gets

5 A 'couch potato' can look _____ than he/she is.
  a older   b younger   c more tired

[/5]

8 Read again and answer the questions.

1 What do many active people do after work?
_____

2 Why are some people bored when they finish school or work? _____

3 What does a 'couch potato' do?
_____

4 How can 'couch potatoes' look?
_____

5 Why are 'couch potatoes' overweight?
_____

[/5]

Listening

9 ⑧ Listen to a radio programme about New York. Tick (✔) true or cross (✗).

1 There are eight million people in New York. ☐
2 People in New York speak 170 languages. ☐
3 The buses are bad in New York. ☐
4 Each year 40 million tourists visit the city. ☐
5 The Statue of Liberty is 93 metres tall. ☐
6 You can buy things in the Statue of Liberty. ☐
7 The Empire State Building has got 112 floors. ☐
8 Many people go jogging in Central Park. ☐
9 There are six universities in New York. ☐
10 Nicolas studies at Columbia University. ☐

[/10]

Are you a couch potato?

Many people take good care of their bodies and have a healthy life. They eat well, keep fit, sleep well and have a good rest after work. They have an active private and professional life.

There are also a lot of people who do not really care about their health. They say that they feel tired after school or work and they are bored because they cannot find anything interesting to do in life. This is when they become 'couch potatoes'.

A 'couch potato' is a child or adult who spends most of his or her free time at home. He or she sits on a couch or lies on a sofa, eats snacks and drinks cola. A couch potato watches lots of TV and often changes the programme to find something better or more interesting. They also watch DVDs or play video games. Sometimes they play the same games all the time.

People who are 'couch potatoes' can look ten years older than people who are healthy and active. Couch potatoes are often overweight because they don't get any physical activity. They only get up from the sofa for something very important. They also get backache because they sit on the sofa for a long time and do not move. Sadly, it is often difficult for them to change their 'couch potato' lifestyle.

Communication

10 Complete the sentences with a word in each gap.

1 A: Have you got any brothers or _____?
   B: Yes, I've got two brothers.

2 A: What's your _____ football team?
   B: Manchester United. I love them!

3 Is your city big or _____?

4 Is there a good bus or train _____?

5 What sports do you _____ on TV?

6 A: Have you got a favourite sports _____?
   B: Yes, it's Ronaldinho.

7 Excuse me, how do I _____ to Victoria Station?

8 Do you _____ to go to the cinema tonight?

9 How _____ do you go to the shopping mall?

10 A: How _____ is a cheese sandwich?
   B: It's £1.60.

[/10]

Marks

Vocabulary and Grammar	/30 marks
Reading	/10 marks
Listening	/10 marks
Communication	/10 marks
Total:	**/60 marks**

Name: ....

Vocabulary & Grammar

1 Choose a name for each category of words below. Then cross out one word in each group which doesn't belong to it.

> music   politics   school subjects
> cooking   places in town   family ✓
> holidays

0 uncle, cousin, wife, ~~friend~~   *family*

1 English, PE, computer, Music   _____

2 cinema, car park, market, bedroom _____

3 mix, invent, cut, boil   _____

4 classical, fireworks, hip-hop, folk   _____

5 droughts, campsite, bed and breakfast, sightseeing   _____

6 vote, government, speech, rope   _____

/6

2 Correct the <u>underlined</u> word in each sentence.

0 Do you have to <u>get dressed</u> a school uniform?
   wear

1 How often do you <u>go</u> basketball? _____

2 I often <u>chat</u> emails to my friends in Spain. _____

3 Put the milk back in the <u>wardrobe</u>. _____

4 I was late for school because my <u>toaster</u> didn't wake me up. It's broken. _____

5 It's <u>foggy</u> today. Take your umbrella. _____

6 My father is a <u>doctor</u> – he looks after sick animals. _____

7 I have a <u>sore</u> in my knee. _____

/7

3 Choose the best word a, b or c to complete the sentences.

0 Your mother's sister is your ____ .
   (a) aunt   b daughter   c grandmother

1 I've got £20 in my ____ .
   a packet   b purse   c mirror

2 You usually buy magazines at the ____ .
   a greengrocer's   b newsagent's   c baker's

3 It's cold today. Don't forget to take a ____ with you.
   a jacket   b dress   c T-shirt

4 We have a lot of ____ here – it rains all the time.
   a wind power   b pollution   c floods

5 Frank often travels ____ train.
   a in   b on   c by

6 I'm really ____ – there's nothing interesting on TV and I don't know what to do.
   a bored   b worried   c nervous

/3

4 Complete the sentences with the correct form of the verbs below.

> be   win   find   wear ✓
> not do   watch   get up

0 Tom *wears* school uniform every day.

1 Robert _____ a lot of tennis matches. He's a great tennis player.

2 I _____ my homework yesterday.

3 Do you think food _____ cheaper next year?

4 I hate _____ at 6 a.m. in the morning.

5 Sarah _____ £10 in the street last Monday.

6 They _____ TV now.

/6

5 <u>Underline</u> the correct answer to complete the sentences.

0 Maria *has*/*have* got two sisters.

1 How *much*/*many* money have you got?

2 I love *the*/*–* tomatoes.

3 We *was*/*were* very tired after school yesterday.

4 Mike is *better*/*best* at Maths than Tom.

5 My birthday is *in*/*on* 24 May.

6 *Are*/*Do* you going to learn Spanish next year?

/3

6 Correct the mistake in each sentence.

0 We are visiting our grandmother every Sunday.
   We visit our grandmother every Sunday.

1 It's not yours pen, it's mine!

_____

2 My grandfather walks very slow.

_____

3 Not you go to the party if you don't like dancing.

_____

4 There is ten girls in my class.

_____

5 Sandra's very happy because she hasn't to wear school uniform.

_____

/5

Reading

7 Read the text. Tick (✔) true or cross (✗).

1 Elizabeth doesn't like London. ☐

2 Elizabeth doesn't want to share her London experience with other people. ☐

3 Elizabeth prepared well to be a tour guide. ☐

4 Elizabeth can answer different tourists' questions. ☐

5 Elizabeth thinks her job is not interesting. ☐

6 Elizabeth says that you don't need to be communicative to be a tour guide. ☐

7 Elizabeth never feels tired at the end of the day. ☐

8 Elizabeth sometimes finds telling the same stories boring. ☐

9 Tourists think Elizabeth is reliable. ☐

10 Elizabeth hasn't got a good sense of humour. ☐

/10

Being a tour guide in London

I'm Elizabeth. I live in London. I know its people, streets and historic places. I also know its palaces and parks, cinemas and theatres and its shopping malls. I love this city. It's one of the busiest cities in the world and it has got the best places to hang out. I am really happy to share my knowledge of London with other people.

I decided to become a tour guide in London. I took some courses, read a lot of books and learnt how to speak clearly and interestingly in public. I think it was a great decision because I know a lot of facts about the city. I can answer almost all the questions tourists ask me about London's nightlife, its dangerous areas and – most of all – its people.

My job is very exciting. You have to have good people skills, be sociable and organised. You have to be a good and caring listener because people often have problems with their accommodation, train tickets or their health. You may need to help them. I am always punctual and start my tours on time, and I love telling creative stories about some parts of the city.

After a day's work, I am often tired – I sometimes repeat the same things and feel a bit bored. But when the tour finishes, people come to thank me for showing them around the city. They tell me I am reliable and have a good sense of humour. This is what really makes me happy about my work.

Listening

8 🔊 Listen to the survey and match the people 1–5 with the electrical objects a–e.

1 Derek   **a** an electric alarm clock
2 Hannah   **b** a mobile phone
3 Anna   **c** an MP3 player
4 Steven   **d** an electric toothbrush
5 Jack   **e** a hairdryer

/5

9 🔊 Listen again and complete the sentences with one word in each gap.

1 Using an electric toothbrush is more convenient and _____ .

2 My hairdryer is quite _____ and silent.

3 I often wonder how people communicated when there weren't any _____ .

4 I like watching movies late at night so I _____ go to sleep after midnight.

5 I got it for my seventeenth _____ .

/5

Communication

10 Complete the mini dialogues with one word in each gap.

1 **A:** Can I have two train _____ to Hastings, please?
   B: Single or _____ ?

2 **A:** What _____ have you got?
   B: I am reliable and I _____ good people skills.

3 **A:** How did you _____ there?
   B: _____ train and then I walked.

4 **A:** Why don't you _____ with us to the disco?
   B: Thanks, that's a good _____ .

5 **A:** What _____ can you speak?
   B: I am fluent _____ English.

/10

Marks	
Vocabulary and Grammar	/30 marks
Reading	/10 marks
Listening	/10 marks
Communication	/10 marks
Total:	**/60 marks**

end of year test

Circle the correct answer a, b, c or d as in the example.

0   I ____ a student.

  a be   **b** am   c is   d are

1   She ___ an electric guitar.

  a have got   b have   c has got   d got

2   I ___ got a camera.

  a not   b don't   c don't have   d haven't

3   My ___ name is David.

  a uncle   b uncle's   c uncles   d uncles'

4   His ____ names are Jacob and Daniel.

  a cousin   b cousin's   c cousins   d cousins'

5   _____ two pens in my bag.

  a There is   b There are   c Are there   d Is there

6   There ____ a café in the park.

  a is   b has   c are   d aren't

7   There are five ___ in my family.

  a child   b child's   c children   d children's

8   I need some money but I haven't got my _____ .

  a mirror   b purse   c inhaler   d ID card

9   Is it his DVD? No, it's ___ .

  a I   b my   c me   d mine

10 He ___ walk to school.

  a isn't   b doesn't   c don't   d hasn't

11 I go to work at 7.30 a.m. and I ___ late in the evening.

  a get home   b wake up   c get dressed
  d have breakfast

12 I get up at 7.00 a.m. every day. I ___ get up at 7.00 a.m.

  a never   b usually   c often   d always

13 Kylie lives with Lauren and Katie but she doesn't talk to ___ .

  a her   b him   c them   d us

14 Do they ___ in the city?

  a live   b to live   c living   d lives

15 There are ____ great shops in my city.

  a a   b some   c any   d much

16 Is there a ___ in the living room?

  a basin   b cooker   c carpet   d sink

17 How ____ rooms are there?

  a a lot of   b some   c much   d many

18 There ____ space for the furniture.

  a isn't much   b isn't many
  c aren't much   d aren't many

19 He can ___ English quite well.

  a to speak   b speak   c speaking   d speaks

20 ___ gymnastics? No, I can't.

  a can you   b Can you do
  c You can do   d Do you

21 I am good at tennis. I can play it ___ .

  a quite   b badly   c very   d well

22 He's a very good swimmer. He swims ___ .

  a fastly   b fast   c faster   d fastest

23 Ellie carries the baby ___ .

  a carefully   b loudly   c clearly   d sadly

24 Can you ___ judo?

  a play   b go   c do   d take

25 Improve your English. ___ a summer course in English!

  a Doing   b Do   c Don't do   d Not do

26 We like ___ pizza.

  a made   b make   c making   d makes

27 I ___ watching football. But I love playing it.

  a love   b hate   c like   d do

28 Tom's favourite snack is _____ .

  a crisps   b tomatoes   c cheese   d meat

29 I like ___ Chinese food.

  a a   b an   c the   d –

30 There's a problem! What's ___ problem?

  a a   b an   c the   d –

31 I take a sandwich and ___ apple to school.

  a a   b an   c the   d –

32 She ___ an exam now.

  a is taking   b takes   c take   d to take

33 Mum's not here. My sister and I ___ dinner today.

  a cook   b cooks   c is cooking   d are cooking

34 Come in! I ___ .

  a don't work   b isn't working
  c 'm not working   d doesn't work

35 What's that music? ___ the piano?

  a They are playing   b Are they playing
  c Do they play   d They play

36 I usually ___ trainers but today I'm wearing boots.

  a am wearing   b wear
  c wears   d wearing

37 Sarah and Fred live in Brighton but at the moment they ___ in an apartment in Venice.

  a stay   b is staying   c stays   d 're staying

38 I've got a _____ in my nose.

  a earrings   b piercing   c belt   d scarf

39 We ___ at the cinema yesterday.

  a are   b was   c is   d were

40 It was a busy day but Jane ___ tired.

  a was   b wasn't   c were   d weren't

41 When you were 10, who ___ your favourite singer?

  a is   b are   c was   d were

42 During the New Year celebrations we watched brilliant _____ in the sky.

    a sweets   b decorations
    c candles   d fireworks

43 Did you stay ___ bed late?

    a on   b in   c at   d to

44 Who ___ you dance with at the party yesterday?

    a do   b did   c are   d were

45 Did they do the shopping on Friday?

    a Yes, they are.   b Yes, they do.
    c Yes, they did.   d Yes, they were.

46 Where did she ___ last holiday?

    a go   b went   c goes   d going

47 I'm sorry, I ___ the letter. I forgot.

    a not read   b don't read
    c didn't read   d am not reading

48 ___ invented the World Wide Web?

    a What   b Who   c When   d Where

49 I can't make phone calls – my mobile needs a _____ .

    a toaster   b cooker   c charger   d player

50 When ___ to Spain? Two years ago.

    a did they go   b they went
    c are they going   d do they go

51 Take an umbrella with you – it's _____ today.

    a foggy   b snowy   c rainy   d windy

52 Walking is ___ for your health.

    a bad   b worse   c good   d better

53 Going by plane is ___ than going by train.

    a expensive   b not expensive
    c more expensive   d most expensive

54 Do you think food will get ___ in the future?

    a cheap   b cheaper   c cheapest d not cheap

55 Who's _____ boy in your class?

    a tall   b taller   c tallest   d the tallest

56 In the next 20 years the global temperature ___ up.

    a is going b goes   c will go   d went

57 _____ study English next year?

    a Are you   b Were you c Will you d Did you

58 I like visiting old towns and cities. I simply love _____ .

    a camping   b walking   c adventure d sightseeing

59 ___ to go bungee jumping at the weekend?

    a Are they going   b Will they go
    c Did they go   d Do they go

60 What is he going to ___ tonight?

    a doing   b do   c did   d does

61 We ___ to stay in a hotel this holiday.

    a not going   b don't go
    c aren't going   d won't go

62 How do you go to work? ___ car.

    a In   b On   c For   d By

63 She _____ wear a uniform at school.

    a have to   b has   c have got d has to

64 ___ work this Saturday?

    a Have you got   b Are you doing
    c Are you going   d Are you having

65 Tom ___ to wear a tie at work.

    a haven't got   b isn't having
    c don't have   d doesn't have

66 A vet

    a talks on the phone.   b sells things.
    c looks after people.   d works with animals.

67 Are you bad ___ remembering things?

    a at   b in   c with   d about

68 If Amanda _____ watching DVDs, invite her to the cinema.

    a like   b likes   c will like
    d is going to like

69 Have you ever ___ to change the world?

    a made   b won   c wanted   d organised

70 I ___ a speech in my life.

    a have ever made   b have never made
    c have never done   d have ever done

71 What ___ when they arrived?

    a are you doing   b do you do   c were you doing   d have you done

72 I was having a shower when Alice _____ .

    a arrived   b was arriving c arrives   d arrive

73 I can't drink this tea. It's ___ !

    a hot enough   b cold enough
    c too hot   d to cold

74 He looks terrible. I think he's got ___ tattoos.

    a too much   b too many
    c not enough   d not too many

75 I _____ to be a lawyer one day.

    a would   b like   c going to d would like

76 My mother's sister is my favourite _____ .

    a niece   b stepmother
    c aunt   d daughter-in-law

77 I don't mind _____ the dishes.

    a wash   b washing   c to wash   d washed

78 He agreed _____ camping.

    a go   b going   c to go   d went

79 Perhaps you _____ leave your car at home and walk more!

    a should   b shouldn't c must   d mustn't

80 You look tired! You ___ get a good night's sleep! It's very important!

    a have   b must   c can   d do

81 Students are ___ to use bad language at school.

   a can't **b** don't have to **c** not allowed **d** shouldn't

82 You ___ watch TV this evening if you do your homework.

   a should **b** must **c** have to **d** can

83 I never make a mess in my room. It's very ____ .

   a stylish **b** dark **c** tidy **d** comfortable

84 It's important not to ___ into trouble.

   a go **b** take **c** have **d** get

85 When I was 16, I ____ allowed to wear make-up.

   a couldn't **b** wasn't **c** didn't **d** didn't have to

86 An accountant has to be

   a good with people. **b** creative.
   c good with numbers. **d** rewarding.

87 Next Friday we ____ to Florida.

   a flies **b** are flying **c** flying **d** to fly

88 My brother ___ home for his summer holiday next month.

   a isn't coming **b** doesn't come
   c didn't come **d** wasn't coming

89 It's possible that the weather will change. It ___ snow tomorrow.

   a can **b** might **c** will **d** should

90 In the future people ___ to live without computers.

   a cannot **b** might not
   c won't be able **d** may not

91 Have you finished your homework ____ ?

   a never **b** yet **c** just **d** ever

92 He has already ____ three matches.

   a win **b** beat **c** won **d** beaten

93 My home is a place ____ I feel really happy.

   a that **b** who **c** which **d** where

94 There hasn't been much rain recently. There is a _____ at the moment

   a flood **b** melting ice
   c hurricanes **d** drought

95 I ____ really frightened of fire when I was little.

   a could be **b** be
   c used to be **d** was used to

96 This book ___ by my favourite author, JRR Tolkien.

   a was written **b** wrote
   c are written **d** has written

97 He's lived here ____ he was born.

   a for **b** ago **c** since **d** ever

98 Has the book been made ____ a film?

   a for **b** into **c** after **d** about

99 If people didn't pay for music, artists ____ records.

   a won't make **b** wouldn't make
   c don't make **d** didn't make

100 He asked me ____ there.

   a go **b** went **c** to go **d** going

audio script

② Language and skills test 1a/1b
exercise 8 and 9 pages 31 and 33

Alex: After school I go home and phone my friend, Jack. We usually meet at 3 o'clock and play football or go skateboarding. Sometimes we watch DVDs at my house or play computer games at Jack's. We love spending time together.

Frank: I wake up very early. I get up at 5.30, and I have breakfast at 6 o'clock. I go to work at 6.30. I always drive my car to work and listen to music on the radio. After work, I often go shopping but I don't like it very much. I get home at about 6 p.m. At 7.30 I have dinner and then, in the evening, I usually read some magazines or send emails to my friends. I go to bed at midnight.

Gina: I always have a good breakfast to start my day. I usually take two sandwiches to work because I am always hungry. I sometimes buy chocolate to eat after my sandwiches. I like chocolate! I have lunch in a café with my friends twice a week. At about 7 p.m. I have dinner and then I relax – I often listen to music.

Martha: I work in a school. I'm a teacher and I like my job. Every day, I teach English and History to my students. I teach six classes every day. I've got a small office with a computer. I often do school work and read books in my office. Sometimes I send emails to other teachers. After school, I teach an evening class at 7 o'clock.

③ Language and skills test 2a/2b
exercise 8 pages 35 and 37

Presenter: Hello, listeners and welcome to the programme! Today we ask four people about the sports they do and their favourite sports personalities. Mike, what sport do you do?

Mike: My favourite sport is football. I think I can play football very well. My favourite players are Ronaldinho and David Beckham. I think they are great players. I play football for a school football team. We meet twice a week – we do exercises and then we play a match.

Presenter: Thank you, Mike. Steven, what about you? Who's your favourite sports person?

Steven: I like Mick Fanning. He's a famous Australian surfer. I can't surf but I love watching the surfers stand on their boards and ride the big waves. It's very exciting to watch them. I often watch surfing competitions on TV.

Presenter: Thanks, Steven. And here's Jodie who loves the mountains.

Jodie: Yes, I do! Climbing mountains is my life but I don't go to the mountains very often. Fortunately, I can practise on a climbing wall. I go to the climbing wall four times a week. I wear a helmet and special shoes, and I use ropes and equipment to climb the wall. My favourite climber is Arlene Blum, a famous American climber. She is now 60 years old but she still enjoys the challenge.

Presenter: Thank you, Jodie. And Georgia, what sport are you good at?

Georgia: Skateboarding, I think. I'm quite good at it and I like it a lot! I think I can do it quite well because I'm good at surfing, and skateboarding is surfing on wheels. We move fast in the skate parks and it's exciting. I always wear knee pads. I don't have a skateboarding hero because in my opinion anyone who tries it is a hero.

④ Listening and skills test 3a/3b
exercise 8 pages 39 and 41

Interviewer: Welcome to our Health and Beauty series on Radio for You. Our guest today is Marie Fiennes. Marie, you are a top model. What do you do to look good?

Marie Fiennes: Hello, everyone. It's nice to be here. Well, there are a lot of things I do but they aren't different from the things everyone does or can do. It's just that I do them regularly. For example, I go for a walk in a nearby park twice a week and I go to the gym every Friday. I like running so I often go running in the morning.

Interviewer: You do a lot of exercise to keep fit – that's very healthy. And what about your diet? What kind of foods do you eat?

Marie Fiennes: I eat food which is good for me. I eat vegetable salads and lots of fruit every day. I like drinking fruit juices – my favourite is orange juice. I don't like drinking coffee because it's bad for me.

Interviewer: Do you eat meat?

Marie Fiennes: No, I don't. I prefer fish. I often have tuna sandwiches for lunch.

Interviewer: I see. Can you cook?

Marie Fiennes: Yes, I think I can. I sometimes cook for my friends.

Interviewer: Marie, what food do you like cooking?

Marie Fiennes: I love French food very much. But when I cook I like using Polish recipes.

Interviewer: So what's your favourite dish from Poland?

Marie Fiennes: All kinds of soups. I love soups. They are delicious, especially mushroom soup.

Interviewer: Marie, the final question – what are you doing in London?

Marie Fiennes: In London? *(laughs)* I'm not working this time. I'm in a cooking competition!

Interviewer: What a surprise! Good luck then! Thank you for coming.

Marie Fiennes: Thanks. Bye.

⑤ Listening and skills test 4a/4b
exercise 7 pages 43 and 45

Presenter: Hello, listeners. I'm Tim Robinson and welcome to our daily programme, *Meet the Genius*. Let me ask some questions for a start: Who drew a picture of the first helicopter? Who painted the *Mona Lisa* and *The Last Supper*? Who was a great engineer and designer? Well, of course, there is one answer to all these questions: Leonardo da Vinci. He was a very intelligent person. Professor Vincent Leonard from Harvard University is our guest today. Professor, what made da Vinci so special?

Professor: Good morning, Tim. Good morning, everyone. First of all, Leonardo was a very talented man. He was a scientist, a painter, an architect, a musician, a botanist… He had a great mind. And he worked hard all his life to develop his abilities.

Interviewer: He was born in Florence, wasn't he?

Professor: Yes, that's right. In 1452. And he also learnt how to paint there. He did his painting in the studio of a famous painter.

Interviewer: What was the painter's name?

Professor: His name was Verocchio.

Interviewer: Did da Vinci live in Florence all his life?

Professor: No, not really. He travelled around Italy: he visited Rome, Bologna and Milan. He also lived in France for some time. That was at the end of his life.

Interviewer: How did he work? Did he do one thing at a time?

Professor: We are not sure about that but I think he simply tried new ideas and different ways of doing things. He was always changing his drawings of machines because he wanted to improve them. He drew many of the first machines that we use today, for example a coffee maker and a keyboard.

Interviewer: That's incredible!

Professor: I absolutely agree.

Interviewer: Did Leonardo get any prizes for his works and inventions during his life time?

Professor: That's an interesting question. Let me think for a moment … Yes, he did. The King of France gave him a house in France. And this was the last house he lived in. He died there at the age of 67. It was in 1519.

Interviewer: What a great man we talked about today! Our guest was Professor Vincent Leonard. Thank you, Professor.

Professor: Thank you.

⑥ Language and skills test 5a/5b
exercise 10 pages 47 and 49

Sarah: Nick, is that you? How nice to see you again!

Nick: Hello, Sarah. What a surprise! How are you doing?

Sarah: I'm fine, thanks. And you?

Nick: Oh, just great. Two days ago I returned from the most beautiful country in the world.

Sarah: That's fantastic! What country are you talking about? Singapore? Thailand?

Nick: No, I'm talking about New Zealand.

Sarah: New Zealand?! That's a long way!

Nick: Well, that's true – it was a long plane journey. The flight took 20 hours but when we landed in Aukland I was really excited, and didn't feel tired.

Sarah: That's good! So how was it?

Nick: It was fantastic – it's not the biggest country in the world, but there are some great places to visit. I went to the North Island and the South Island. You know, the country of New Zealand has two main islands.

Sarah: I see. So what did you do there? What type of holiday was it?

Nick: Well, it was a walking holiday. We walked up some beautiful mountains and the weather was warm and sunny. We found some great campsites too, and met some new friends.

Sarah: What was the best bit?

Nick: The best thing was travelling by different means of transport – we went on mountain bikes, by kayak across a river and walked a lot, too.

Sarah: And what was the worst bit?

Nick: The worst bit was when we went kayaking. It was late in the evening and water started to go in my sister's kayak. Fortunately, she rowed back to our camp, but she was very cold and didn't feel well.

Sarah: Oh, dear. Was the weather good?

Nick: Yes, it was sunny all the time and there were only three rainy days with some fog.

Sarah: Nick, you are so lucky.

Nick: I know … And I'm going on another trip to New Zealand next summer. Why don't you come with me?

Sarah: Really? Thanks, Nick. I'll think about it.

Nick: Okay, then. I'll give you a ring soon.

Sarah: Yes, thanks. Bye for now, Nick.

⑦ Language and skills test 6a/6b
exercise 9 pages 51 and 53

Presenter: I asked some teenagers about the jobs they want to do in the future. Here's what they said. First, Marco.

Marco: I am thinking about working as a teacher. My mum is an English teacher. I want to be a Maths teacher and I'd like to work with children. I think it's a fascinating job but also very difficult. I know teaching is not easy! You have to be good with kids, be organised and caring – I think I am – and you have to speak clearly. The good thing about being a teacher is that you don't have to work all year round and you have lots of holidays!

Presenter: Jasmin, what about you?

Jasmin: I want to be a vet. I have got three cats and two dogs at home. When they are ill, I always take them to the vet and I watch carefully what the vet is doing. I'm going to get a voluntary job at the vet's this summer. I think I will learn a lot just by helping with the sick animals.

Presenter: Peter, what job do you want?

Peter: I want to be a police officer. I have always wanted to do this job. To be a good police officer, you have to be strong, quick and fit. It is a job with lots of responsibility. You can't be a nervous person! But I think I have the right skills to do the job well. I have a clear list of goals and I know I'll be a good police officer!

Presenter: And finally, Sheila.

Sheila: A hairdresser, of course. I have always wanted to be one. I'm interested in fashion. I think I'm creative and I like trying out new hairstyles. To be a good hairdresser you have to be polite and be a good listener. You also have to be reliable. People like to relax when they sit for an hour or two at the hairdresser's – so it's good to have a sense of humour, too.

8 Midyear test

exercise 9, page 59

Presenter: Welcome to our weekly programme, *Famous cities of the world*. Today, our guest, Nicolas Ferguson, is talking about New York. Nicolas, do you live in New York?

Nicolas: Hello, listeners. Yes, I do. I also study there and I think it is a fascinating city.

Presenter: What's special about New York?

Nicolas: Well, first of all, it is a very big interesting city. It has got a population of eight million people and 36 percent are from other countries. Do you know that people in New York speak 170 languages?

Presenter: That's amazing – I didn't know that! So how do people move around the city?

Nicolas: New York is a busy city – some people say it's a city that never sleeps. There is a lot of traffic on the roads but there are good buses and a subway.

Presenter: I see. Forty-seven million foreign and American tourists visit New York every year. What can they do in New York?

Nicolas: Oh, lots of things. There are many famous museums and art galleries, for example, the Metropolitan Museum of Art. There are also famous monuments like the Statue of Liberty. It is 93 metres tall and there is a museum inside. You can buy gifts there, like postcards, DVDs and small models. New York is famous for its very high buildings like the Empire State Building and the Bank of America Tower.

Presenter: How tall are they?

Nicolas: The Empire State Building has got 102 floors! I'm not sure about the Bank of America.

Presenter: Is New York a green city?

Nicolas: Yes, it is very green. There are many parks in New York, for example Central Park in Manhattan. New Yorkers love walking in the parks, and many of them go jogging there.

Presenter: How about shopping in New York?

Nicolas: It's a great city for shoppers. There are lots of shopping malls with good quality goods and exciting restaurants with food from all over the world, cinemas or places to sit and relax. But I don't have much time to do these things. I have a lot of university work to do.

Presenter: What university do you study at?

Nicolas: Well, there are ten universities and I study Art at Columbia University.

Presenter: Good luck with your studies then. Thank you very much.

Nicolas: Thank you.

9 End of year test

exercises 8 and 9, page 61

Interviewer: It is impossible for modern man to live without electricity. We all use many electrical devices at work and at home. I have asked five people about the objects they use every day. Derek?

Derek: The first thing I do when I wake up is go to the bathroom and clean my teeth. I don't use a normal toothbrush. I use an electric toothbrush. My dentist says that electric toothbrushes are more convenient and healthier. At first I wasn't sure about using it every day but now I like it.

Interviewer: Thank you. And now, Hannah, what electrical device do you use?

Hannah: I can't imagine living without my hairdryer. After I wash my hair I have to dry it very quickly. I know that drying your hair isn't good for your hair's condition but I am very impatient and I don't like it when my hair is wet. My hairdryer is quite small and silent so I can take it with me wherever I go.

Interviewer: Anna, what do you use every day?

Anna: A mobile phone, of course. It's one of the most useful and important electrical objects I can think of. I use it at work and I call my relatives and friends when I need to. It's fast. I often wonder how people communicated when there weren't any phones. It's really hard to imagine!

Interviewer: Yes, it is. Steven? What is the most useful electrical object for you?

Steven: You may be surprised but it's an electric alarm clock. I use it every day. I find it very hard to wake up in the morning. You know, I like watching movies late at night so I often go to sleep after midnight. I have to arrive at the office on time so I set the alarm clock half an hour earlier to be sure I'm not late for work.

Interviewer: And you, Jack?

Jack: I use lots of electrical objects. My favourite is a new MP3 player. I got it for my seventeenth birthday. It stores hundreds of songs and I can listen to it all the time. It's a truly great invention.

audio script

Short test 1a Unit 1

1 1 c, 2 a, 3 a, 4 b
2 1 bicycle, 2 mobile, 3 skateboard, 4 keys, 5 wallet,
6 tissues
3 1 fair, 2 friendly, 3 short, 4 beard
4 1 Peter hasn't got/has not got a DVD player. 2 We've
got/have got three TVs in our house. 3 Have you got a
boyfriend? 4 I haven't got/have not got a moustache.
5 1 There are, 2 Is there, 3 There aren't
6 1 grandparents', 2 people, 3 your, 4 Tom's, 5 man, 6 ours

Short test 1b Unit 1

1 1 b, 2 c, 3 a, 4 a
2 1 camera, 2 console, 3 guitar, 4 earphones, 5 mirror,
6 chewing
3 1 short, 2 shy, 3 fair, 4 moustache
4 1 Robert hasn't got/has not got a beard. 2 They've got/
have got two DVD players in their house. 3 I haven't got/
have not got a skateboard. 4 Have you got a girlfriend?
5 1 There aren't, 2 There are, 3 Is there
6 1 mine, 2 Olivia's, 3 their, 4 women, 5 friends', 6 person

Short test 2a Unit 2

1 1 c, 2 g, 3 a, 4 f, 5 b, 6 d
2 1 History, 2 Foreign, 3 Science, 4 Music, 5 Technology
3 1 c, 2 a, 3 a, 4 b, 5 c, 6 b
4 1 She gets up at 8 a.m. on Mondays. 2 Robert's girlfriend
watches TV every day. 3 He doesn't go to school by bus.
4 Hannah's brother has lunch at school. 5 Mrs Smith
doesn't visit her grandmother on Tuesdays.
5 1 How often do they play tennis? 2 What time does
she wake up on Sundays?/When does she wake up on
Sundays? 3 How do you spell 'geography'? 4 Where do
you live?

Short test 2b Unit 2

1 1 g, 2 b, 3 d, 4 f, 5 a, 6 c
2 1 Geography, 2 Design, 3 Citizenship, 4 Education,
5 English
3 1 a, 2 b, 3 b, 4 a, 5 c, 6 c
4 1 She doesn't listen to music every day. 2 Tom does his
homework at school. 3 Our Maths lesson doesn't start
at 11 a.m. 4 My brother studies History. 5 Joan walks to
school with her best friend.
5 1 How often do they go to the cinema? 2 What do you
have for breakfast? 3 Where do her parents work? 4
What time does Caroline usually get up?/When does
Caroline usually get up?

Short test 3a Unit 3

1 **Shops:** pharmacy, clothes shop, greengrocer's
Rooms in the house: bedroom, kitchen, bathroom
Places in town: library, post office, car park
Things at home: armchair, wardrobe, sink
2 1 polluted, 2 great, 3 beautiful, 4 interesting
3 1 b, 2 c, 3 a, 4 a
4 1 many, 2 a lot of, 3 much, 4 much, 5 many, 6 a lot of
5 1 There's a park near my house – it's really nice! 2 How
many girls are there in your class? 3 There isn't a TV in
this room. 4 There are many clothes in my wardrobe.
5 There aren't any hotels in my town./There are some
hotels in my town.

Short test 3b Unit 3

1 **Places in town:** town hall, fire station, stadium
Things at home: cooker, basin, carpet
Rooms in the house: living room, bedroom, kitchen
Shops: baker's, bookshop, newsagent's
2 1 terrible, 2 famous, 3 brilliant, 4 exciting
3 1 b, 2 c, 3 a, 4 c
4 1 a lot of, 2 many, 3 much, 4 a lot of, 5 much, 6 many
5 1 There is a lot of space in my bedroom. 2 There aren't
any swimming pools in my town./There are some
swimming pools in my town. 3 There's a great market
near my house – I often go there. 4 Is there much/a lot of
rain in your city? 5 We haven't got a washing machine in
our house.

Short test 4a Unit 4

1 1 b, 2 a, 3 b, 4 c
2 1 head, 2 arm, 3 finger, 4 knee, 5 foot
3 1 toothache, 2 cough, 3 sore
4 1 Can your brother dance? 2 My sister can't/cannot cycle
very well. 3 They can play rugby quite well.
5 1 loudly, 2 terribly, 3 hard, 4 slowly, 5 well
6 1 Don't touch, 2 Go, 3 Don't, 4 Don't speak

Short test 4b Unit 4

1 1 a, 2 a, 3 c, 4 b
2 1 back, 2 shoulder, 3 elbow, 4 leg, 5 toe
3 1 pain, 2 backache, 3 cold
4 1 Bob and Tricia can dance quite well. 2 I can't/cannot
ride a horse well. 3 Can your girlfriend play computer
games?
5 1 carefully, 2 clearly, 3 fast, 4 quietly, 5 easily
6 1 Don't eat, 2 Watch, 3 Go, 4 Don't wait

Short test 5a Unit 5

1 1 the lettuce, 2 the oil, 3 the green beans into pieces
2 1 vegetable, 2 juice, 3 crisps, 4 rice, 5 bananas,
6 cereal
3 1 Tom hates watching football on TV. 2 I don't like
wearing school uniform. 3 Do they like visiting relatives?
4 She loves hanging out with friends.
5 Does your sister like going to bed early?
4 1 c, 2 b, 3 b, 4 a
5 1 There is a sofa in the living room. 2 His wife is a chef
and works in a restaurant. 3 I never buy clothes in a
supermarket. 4 My brother's an actor and my sister's a
doctor.

Short test 5b Unit 5

1 1 the apples into pieces, 2 the cheese, 3 the juice
2 1 milk, 2 fish, 3 biscuits, 4 cereal, 5 fruit, 6 pizza
3 1 Mary loves cooking Chinese food. 2 Does your teacher
like listening to music? 3 We don't like helping at home.
4 Do they like watching sport on TV? 5 I love reading
books about the past.
4 1 b, 2 a, 3 c, 4 c
5 1 I have a sandwich and an apple for lunch. 2 I often
buy magazines at a newsagent's. 3 There is a cooker in
the kitchen. 4 Her husband's a doctor and works in a
hospital.

Short test 6a Unit 6

1 1 ✗, 2 ✔, 3 ✗, 4 ✔

2 1 password, 2 chat, 3 pages, 4 download, 5 send, 6 online

3 1 Are you writing to Sam? 2 They are not waiting for the teacher. 3 What is Nick drinking? 4 Dave and Ian are running very fast.

4 1 are you doing, 2 do you walk, 3 's not sleeping, 4 have

5 1 go, 2 wear, 3 's/is peeling, 4 'm/am studying, 5 Are they talking, 6 doesn't/does not play

Short test 6b Unit 6

1 1 ✔, 2 ✔, 3 ✗, 4 ✗

2 1 create, 2 messaging, 3 log, 4 blog, 5 username, 6 research

3 1 What is Jessica eating? 2 Georgia and Beth are singing very loudly. 3 Are you talking to me? 4 We are not listening to Luke.

4 1 'm not doing, 2 cycle, 3 are you reading, 4 do you eat

5 1 has, 2 'm/am going, 3 doesn't/does not like, 4 're/are playing, 5 's/is talking, 6 wake

Short test 7a Unit 7

1 1 rock, 2 folk, 3 classical, 4 disco, 5 hip-hop

2 1 ✗, 2 ✔, 3 ✗, 4 ✔

3 1 The weather was terrible yesterday. 2 Where were Paul and John last night? 3 We weren't/were not tired after our PE lesson. 4 Was the concert good?

4 Regular verbs
celebrate – celebrated, cook – cooked
Irregular verbs
go – went, wear – wore

5 1 started, 2 had, 3 sent, 4 stayed , 5 gave

Short test 7b Unit 7

1 1 jazz, 2 pop, 3 heavy metal, 4 classical, 5 disco

2 1 ✗, 2 ✗, 3 ✔, 4 ✔

3 1 Where were you last Monday? 2 Her cousins weren't/were not friendly. 3 Was the film interesting? 4 I was at the cinema last weekend.

4 Regular verbs
decorate – decorated, start – started
Irregular verbs
give – gave, have – had

5 1 went, 2 finished, 3 put, 4 wore, 5 tidied

Short test 8a Unit 8

1 1 hairdryer, 2 cooker, 3 player, 4 charger, 5 kettle

2 1 b, 2 c, 3 a, 4 b

3 1 Did they go to the cinema last weekend? 2 Did Becky and Helen have a good time on holiday? 3 We didn't eat pizza yesterday. 4 Did your cousin send you an email last week? 5 I didn't see our English teacher at school yesterday. 6 The children didn't wake up very late on Saturday.

4 1 What did he wear? 2 Where did they go? 3 Who did she visit? 4 How many books did you read? 5 When did they finish work?

5 1 created, 2 did Laszlo Biro invent, 3 closed, 4 did you go

Short test 8b Unit 8

1 1 toaster, 2 charger, 3 radio, 4 alarm, 5 toothbrush

2 1 b, 2 c, 3 a, 4 c

3 1 I didn't make breakfast for my family yesterday. 2 Did Sam ride his bicycle to school on Monday? 3 We didn't watch the match on TV last night. 4 Did you go to school

yesterday? 5 Did Peter's parents sell their house last year? 6 I didn't text my boyfriend at the weekend.

4 1 How many films did you watch at the weekend? 2 What time did they wake up? 3 Who did Sandra see yesterday? 4 Where did John's grandparents live? 5 What did Mrs Smith give you?

5 1 did you meet, 2 opened, 3 did Karl Benz design, 4 painted *The Sunflowers*

Short test 9a Unit 9

1 Weather: windy, sunny
Environmental problems: pollution, hurricanes
Recyclable rubbish: bottles, plastic
Solutions to local problems: litter bins, green spaces

2 1 droughts, 2 cloudy, 3 Global, 4 packaging

3 1 nicer, 2 more interesting, 3 worse, 4 greener

4 1 Our teacher/My best friend is taller than my best friend/teacher. 2 History/Geography is more difficult than Geography/History. 3 Apples are healthier than sweets. 4 My mobile phone/My friend's mobile phone is better than my friend's mobile phone/mine.

5 1 It won't be sunny tomorrow. 2 Where will you be in ten years? 3 There won't be enough oil in the future. 4 The price of vegetables will go down next year.

Short test 9b Unit 9

1 Weather: rainy, foggy
Environmental problems: global warming, droughts
Recyclable rubbish: packaging, batteries
Solutions to local problems: traffic-free zones, public transport

2 1 Hurricanes, 2 sunny, 3 Pollution, 4 cycle lanes

3 1 better, 2 bigger, 3 more polluted, 4 cleaner

4 1 London/Paris is more beautiful than Paris/London. 2 My computer/My friend's computer is worse than my friend's computer/mine. 3 Maths/Science is easier than Science/Maths. 4 Our teacher/My best friend is shorter than my best friend/teacher.

5 1 It won't be stormy tomorrow. 2 The price of clothes will go up next year. 3 There won't be much rain in the future. 4 Where will she live in five years?

Short test 10a Unit 10

1 1 by, 2 on, 3 by, 4 by

2 Types of holiday: sightseeing
Places to stay: apartment
Transport: helicopter

3 1 ✗, 2 ✔, 3 ✗, 4 ✔

4 1 We're/are going to play football tomorrow after school. 2 What are you going to do at the weekend? 3 I'm not/am not going to go to the mountains this winter. 4 Tom and Robert aren't/are not going to come to my birthday party next Saturday. 5 Is Sarah going to visit her grandmother in hospital today?

5 1 the tallest, 2 the prettiest, 3 the most beautiful, 4 the best

6 1 What was the worst film you watched on TV last week? 2 Who's the most popular actor in your country? 3 What's the smallest room in your house? 4 What's the most expensive car in the world?

Short test 10b Unit 10

1 1 by, 2 by, 3 on, 4 by

2 Transport: ship
Places to stay: campsite
Types of holiday: adventure

3 1 ✗, 2 ✔, 3 ✗, 4 ✔
4 1 I'm/am going to study for my History test at the weekend. 2 Georgia and Debbie aren't/are not going to go to the cinema with us next Friday. 3 Is Tom going to play basketball with us today after school? 4 We aren't/are not going to watch TV this evening. 5 What time are you going to get up tomorrow?
5 1 the hottest, 2 the most intelligent, 3 the busiest, 4 the worst
6 1 What's the most beautiful place you know? 2 Who's the happiest person in your family? 3 Who's the best singer in the world? 4 What was the most interesting film you watched on TV last week?

Short test 11a Unit 11
1 1 f, 2 d, 3 b, 4 a, 5 g, 6 c
2 1 vet, 2 memory, 3 organised, 4 assistant, 5 worried, 6 nurse
3 1 surprised, 2 reliable, 3 happy, 4 patient
4 1 at, 2 on, 3 on, 4 at, 5 In, 6 on, 7 in, 8 at
5 1 has to get up, 2 Do you have to send, 3 doesn't have to help, 4 don't have to wear, 5 do I have to do

Short test 11b Unit 11
1 1 b, 2 a, 3 c, 4 d, 5 g, 6 f
2 1 upset, 2 clerk, 3 nervous, 4 officer, 5 sense, 6 driver
3 1 bored, 2 independent, 3 polite, 4 sad
4 1 in, 2 at, 3 on, 4 at, 5 on, 6 at, 7 in, 8 on
5 1 do you have to pay, 2 don't have to work, 3 has to help, 4 Do we have to read, 5 doesn't have to share

Short test 12a Unit 12
1 1 greet, 2 vote, 3 receive, 4 organise
2 1 government, 2 blow, 3 voters, 4 crime, 5 speech
3 **Regular verbs:** talk – talked, help – helped
Irregular verbs: drive – driven, think – thought
4 1 Robert has/'s never won any tennis matches. 2 Have Hannah and Bethany ever downloaded music from the internet? 3 I have/'ve never visited my aunt in Germany. 4 Has Sue ever been to Mexico? 5 You have/'ve never played rugby.
5 1 e If you are hungry, eat an apple. 2 a If you feel tired, don't go to bed late. 3 b If you see Joan tomorrow, say hello to her. 4 d If you like Peter, don't forget his birthday next week.

Short test 12b Unit 12
1 1 blow, 2 offer, 3 bow, 4 make
2 1 protested, 2 receive, 3 Bullying, 4 government, 5 elections
3 **Regular verbs:** want – wanted, sign – signed
Irregular verbs: speak – spoken, wear – worn
4 1 Have your parents ever been to San Francisco? 2 I have/'ve never cycled to school. 3 Has Mrs Brown ever walked to work? 4 Chris has/'s never swum in the sea. 5 You have/'ve never cooked lunch for your family.
5 1 d If you see Paul tomorrow, invite him to my birthday party. 2 a If you are cold, put on a sweater. 3 e If you have a pain in your leg, don't play football. 4 b If you chat on the internet, don't give your real name and address.

Language and skills test 1a Units 1&2
1 **My family:** parents, aunt, husband
My things: mirror, packet of tissues, keys
School subjects: Maths, ICT, Citizenship
Describing people: tall, good-looking, shy

2 1 walk, 2 listen, 3 have, 4 go, 5 watch
3 1 How often do you hang out with friends? 2 My mother goes shopping once a week. 3 I usually get dressed after breakfast. 4 My sister doesn't help at home.
4 1 children, 2 Have, 3 mine, 4 Sandra's, 5 There are, 6 him
5 1 What time does she wake up? 2 There are three women in my family./There is one woman in my family. 3 My best friend doesn't have/hasn't got a mobile phone. 4 Does your sister often talk with her friends?
6 1 b, 2 a, 3 a, 4 b, 5 c, 6 c
7 1 ✔, 2 ✔, 3 ✗, 4 ✔, 5 ✗, 6 ✗, 7 ✔, 8 ✔
8 1 c, 2 d, 3 b, 4 a
9 1 At 3 o'clock, 2 He drives a car./By car. 3 She listens to music. 4 She does school work and reads books. She sends emails.
10 1 This, meet, 2 Where, in, 3 hope, 4 first, 5 soon, 6 favourite, course

Language and skills test 1b Units 1&2
1 **Describing people:** short, slim, friendly
My things: wallet, sunglasses, lip salve
My family: uncle, wife, daughter
School subjects: PE, Geography, Design and Technology
2 1 do, 2 read, 3 go, 4 have, 5 do
3 1 She goes to the cinema twice a month. 2 Her brother doesn't wear school uniform. 3 How often do they go to school by bus? 4 I often hang out with my friends.
4 1 your, 2 us, 3 grandparents', 4 child, 5 Have, 6 Is there
5 1 We don't have/haven't got a pet. 2 Does your sister often help at home? 3 When does Tom listen to music? 4 There is a man in the park./There are men in the park.
6 1 c, 2 a, 3 b, 4 c, 5 b, 6 a
7 1 ✗, 2 ✗, 3 ✔, 4 ✔, 5 ✗, 6 ✗, 7 ✔, 8 ✔
8 1 c, 2 b, 3 d, 4 a
9 1 At Alex's house. 2 Franks does the shopping. 3 At 7 pm. 4 Six classes a day.
10 1 How, 2 for, 3 Hello/Hi, meet, 4 in, I'm, 5 fine, here, 6 name

Language and skills test 2a Units 3&4
1 1 news, 2 post, 3 running, 4 gymnastics
2 **Sports:** volleyball, **Body:** leg, **In town:** hospital, **Shops:** pharmacy, **Illnesses:** sore, **Rooms:** bathroom
3 1 terrible, 2 brilliant, 3 famous, 4 polluted
4 1 Can your teacher play the piano? 2 I can't cycle very well. 3 Can you play badminton well? 4 Lee and Mark/Mark and Lee can swim well.
5 1 Don't touch, 2 quickly, 3 a, 4 many, 5 Open, 6 happy, 7 many, 8 any
6 1 play, 2 climbing, 3 can, 4 many, 5 any
7 1 b, 2 c, 3 a, 4 c, 5 b, 6 b, 7 c, 8 b
8 1 ✔, 2 ✗, 3 ✗, 4 ✔, 5 ✗, 6 ✔, 7 ✗, 8 ✔
9 1 How do I get to the museum? 2 Is the Starlight Cinema near here? 3 Have you got a favourite football team? 4 Is your town big or small? 5 Do you do any sports?
10 1 take, 2 go, 3 See, 4 say

Language and skills test 2b Units 3&4
1 1 green, 2 sick, 3 karate, 4 baseball
2 **Extreme sports:** climbing, **Parts of the body:** finger, **In town:** office, **Shops:** baker's, **Illnesses:** pain, **In the kitchen:** cooker
3 1 famous, 2 exciting, 3 polluted, 4 terrible

4 1 He can't play golf very well. 2 Imogen and Ruth/Ruth and Imogen can sing well. 3 Can your parents dance the samba? 4 Can you ride a motorbike well?

5 1 good, 2 any, 3 Close, 4 any, 5 much, 6 Don't run, 7 many, 8 safely

6 1 can, 2 play, 3 surfboard, 4 much, 5 any

7 1 c, 2 a, 3 b, 4 b, 5 a, 6 a, 7 c, 8 a

8 1 ✗, 2 ✔, 3 ✗, 4 ✗, 5 ✗, 6 ✔, 7 ✗, 8 ✔

9 1 Can you say that again, please? 2 How do I get to the National Bank? 3 What can you do in the evenings? 4 What sports do you (usually) watch on TV? 5 Is there a good bus or train service?

10 1 at, 2 meet, 3 Here's/There's, 4 miss

Language and skills test 3a Units 5&6

1 (marks for each item indicated in answers)
Food: tomatoes (0.5) , biscuits (0.5), eggs (1), onions (1)
Clothes: dress (0.5), shirt (0.5), sweater (1), hoodie (1)
The internet: username (0.5), blogs (0.5) , page (1), download (1)

2 1 vegetable, 2 belt, 3 cut, 4 chatting

3 1 I love playing basketball. 2 Maria's/is having breakfast now. 3 What time do you usually get up? 4 My little sister doesn't/does not like helping at home. 5 Robert does karate three times a week. 6 The teacher's/is speaking to us.

4 1 an, 2 the, 3 a, 4 –, 5 The

5 1 a, 2 c, 3 b, 4 a, 5 a, 6 c

6 1 c, 2 d, 3 a, 4 b

7 1 You can buy products which you cannot find in a normal shop, and they are often cheaper. 2 prices of (their favourite singers' or bands' new) CDs and DVDs, 3 cool, 4 That they often change.

8 1 top, 2 Friday, 3 running, 4 orange, 5 cooks, 6 Polish, 7 delicious, 8 cooking

9 1 like, much, Anything, 2 would, have, please, 3 want, idea, 4 sure

Language and skills test 3b Units 5&6

1 (marks for each item indicated in answers)
Clothes: trousers (0.5), boots (0.5), trainers (1), jacket (1)
The internet: chatroom (0.5), download (0.5), password (1), log (1)
Food: meat (0.5), cereal (0.5), fish (1), bananas (1)

2 1 sweater, 2 the potatoes, 3 research, 4 fruit

3 1 Don't talk so loudly! The baby's/is sleeping. 2 They don't/do not like getting up early. 3 Jane's/is reading a book at the moment. 4 What do you usually have for lunch? 5 I hate watching football on TV. 6 Tim goes skiing twice a year.

4 1 The, 2 –, 3 the, 4 a, 5 an

5 1 a, 2 c, 3 a, 4 b, 5 c, 6 b

6 1 c, 2 a, 3 b, 4 d

7 1 because it's fast and easy, 2 for music and games (and MP3 players), 3 at a party, 4 young people's likes and dislikes

8 1 twice, 2 fruit, 3 coffee, 4 tuna, 5 French, 6 Poland, 7 mushroom, 8 cooking

9 1 piece, Here, That 2 juice, How, change 3 join, can't 4 agree

Language and skills test 4a Units 7&8

1 1 classical, 2 candles, 3 invented, 4 alarm, 5 jazz, 6 cards

2 1 kettle, 2 radio, 3 clothes, 4 designed, 5 easily

3 1 were, 2 woke up, 3 didn't go, 4 didn't enjoy, 5 sent

4 1 I didn't wear my school uniform yesterday. 2 Who created Facebook? 3 My father gave me £10 two days ago. 4 Who did you go with to the party on Saturday? 5 Why was Hannah unhappy last night? 6 They were very tired yesterday after school.

5 1 a, 2 b, 3 b, 4 a, 5 c, 6 c

6 1 ✔, 2 ✔, 3 ✗, 4 ✗, 5 ✔, 6 ✗, 7 ✔, 8 ✔

7 1 Every day, 2 Harvard, 3 In Florence, 4 A painter (da Vinci's teacher), 5 Rome, Bologna and Milan, 6 many of the first machines that we use today, for example, a helicopter, a coffee maker and a keyboard, 7 a house in France, 8 In (his house in) France

8 1 Where did you have lunch? 2 Who did you go with? 3 Did you enjoy it?

9 1 e, 2 a, 3 d, 4 g, 5 f, 6 b, 7 c

Language and skills test 4b Units 7&8

1 1 special, 2 player, 3 hip-hop, 4 heavy, 5 dancing, 6 designed

2 1 radio, 2 charger, 3 discovered, 4 TV/television, 5 mobile

3 1 didn't go, 2 gave, 3 didn't have, 4 was, 5 sold

4 1 I woke up many times last night. 2 Who did you go with to the cinema last night? 3 I didn't send him an email yesterday. 4 Who made the first mobile phone call? 5 Where were you last night? 6 Robert was in London three years ago.

5 1 c, 2 a, 3 c, 4 b, 5 a, 6 b

6 1 ✔, 2 ✔, 3 ✗, 4 ✗, 5 ✗, 6 ✔, 7 ✔, 8 ✗

7 1 A professor at Harvard University, 2 In 1452, 3 a painter/da Vinci's teacher, 4 Italy, 5 because he wanted to improve them, 6 the King of France, 7 In France, 8 67

8 1 Where did you go? 2 What did you do there? 3 How did you get there?

9 1 g, 2 c, 3 a, 4 d, 5 e, 6 b, 7 f

Language and skills test 5a Units 9&10

1 1 snow, 2 campsite, 3 foot, 4 environment

2 1 apartment, 2 by, 3 floods, 4 windy

3 1 packaging, 2 foggy, 3 batteries, 4 spaces

4 1 the most beautiful, 2 better, 3 cheaper, 4 the messiest, 5 more interesting

5 1 is/'s going to be, 2 Are you going to go, 3 are/'re going to travel, 4 am/'m not going to wear

6 1 Will it be cold tomorrow? 4 I think Sarah won't be at school tomorrow. 5 I think the weather will be good tomorrow.

7 1 hotel, 2 sunny, 3 sightseeing, 4 more expensive, 5 are, 6 will

8 1 bike, 2 school, 3 money, 4 packaging

9 1 She cycles/rides a bike. 2 They recycle it. 3 low-energy light bulbs, 4 plastic bags

10 1 a, 2 b, 3 c, 4 b, 5 c, 6 b, 7 b, 8 b

11 1 for, 2 over, 3 like, 4 different, 5 try, 6 What, 7 bigger, 8 better, 9 take

Language and skills test 5b Units 9&10

1 1 campsite, 2 wind, 3 pollution, 4 inline skates

2 1 boat, 2 on, 3 droughts, 4 by

3 1 rubbish, 2 lanes, 3 kayak, 4 apartment

4 1 bigger, 2 more difficult, 3 the most intelligent, 4 the greatest, 5 better

5 1 Are you going to wear, **2** am/'m going to be, **3** is not/isn't going to join, **4** are/'re going to play

6 **2** What will the weather be like tomorrow?
3 My father won't be home at Christmas,
5 I will go to university in the future.

7 1 breakfast, **2** stormy, **3** better, **4** aren't, **5** beach, **6** will

8 1 cycles/rides a bike, **2** turn/switch, **3** packaged, **4** environment

9 1 by bus, **2** They recycle it. **3** They always turn off the taps. **4** fast food

10 1 c, **2** b, **3** a, **4** b, **5** c, **6** a, **7** a, **8** c

11 1 list, **2** need, **3** looking, **4** there, **5** on, **6** sorry, **7** smaller, **8** better, **9** take

Language and skills test 6a
Units 11&12

1 (marks for each item indicated in answers)
Jobs: photographer (0.5), teacher (0.5), worker (1), police (1)
Feelings: surprised (0.5), happy (0.5), bored (1), tired (1)
Politics: government (0.5), make a speech (0.5), elections (1), crime (1)

2 1 bow, **2** patient, **3** after people

3 1 in, **2** on, **3** on, **4** at, **5** at, **6** in

4 1 We haven't found any interesting books in the school library. **2** I've never driven a car because I'm only 15. **3** Has Eddie ever argued with his grandmother? **4** They have never flown a plane.

5 1 don't, **2** Do you have, **3** don't have, **4** go

6 1 sense, **2** have, **3** at, **4** Don't

7 1 c, **2** b, **3** a, **4** b

8 1 by plane, **2** an old wooden house, **3** because it is expensive to park in the city centre, **4** a large theme park

9 1 d/g, **2** b/h, **3** a/f, **4** c/e

10 1 Where are you from? **2** What skills and qualities have you got? **3** What languages do you speak? **4** What are your favourite subjects at school?

11 1 Sir, **2** apply, **3** Yours, **4** work, **5** skills

Language and skills test 6b
Units 11&12

1 (marks for each item indicated in answers)
Feelings: nervous (0.5), upset (0.5), worried (1), angry (1)
Politics: parliament (0.5), politicians (0.5), voters (1), speech (1)
Jobs: nurse (0.5), hairdresser (0.5), driver (1), assistant (1)

2 1 people, **2** greet, **3** after children

3 1 at, **2** on, **3** in, **4** on, **5** at, **6** at

4 1 I want to go to Paris next year because I've never been there. **2** Has your brother ever helped you with your French homework? **3** We have never spoken about it. **4** My parents haven't met my History teacher.

5 1 doesn't have to, **2** don't, **3** Do you have to, **4** stay

6 1 take, **2** have, **3** tired, **4** Don't

7 1 b, **2** a, **3** c, **4** c

8 1 Dutch paintings by Rembrandt, **2** well organised, **3** 1470, **4** went on the rides and relaxed in cafés

9 1 c/g, **2** a/f, **3** d/h, **4** b/e

10 1 Why do you want this job? **2** What languages do you speak? **3** What skills have you got? **4** Have you got any questions?

11 1 contact, **2** Yours, **3** forward, **4** sense, **5** speak

Midyear test

1 1 sport, **2** health, **3** shops, **4** food, **5** clothes, **6** home,

2 1 go, **2** feel, **3** do, **4** cut, **5** log, **6** have, **7** go

3 1 b, **2** a, **3** b, **4** c, **5** c, **6** a

4 1 create, **2** doesn't drink, **3** are playing, **4** don't walk, **5** going, **6** visit

5 1 well, **2** my, **3** friend's, **4** them, **5** many, **6** children

6 1 I always get up at 7 o'clock. **2** My mother's a teacher. **3** Does Tom like playing badminton? **4** How many sisters has Patricia got? **5** There isn't any milk in the fridge.

7 1 a, **2** b, **3** c, **4** b, **5** a

8 1 They have a good rest. **2** Because they cannot find anything interesting to do in life. **3** A 'couch potato' sits on a couch or lies on a sofa, eats snacks and drinks cola, watches lots of TV, DVDs or plays video games. **4** 'Couch potatoes' can look ten years older than people who are healthy and active. **5** Because they don't get enough physical activity.

9 1 ✔, **2** ✔, **3** ✗, **4** ✗, **5** ✔, **6** ✔, **7** ✗, **8** ✔, **9** ✗, **10** ✔

10 1 sisters, **2** favourite, **3** small, **4** service, **5** watch, **6** personality, **7** get, **8** want, **9** often, **10** much

End of year test

1 1 school subjects – computer, **2** places in town – bedroom, **3** cooking – invent, **4** music – fireworks, **5** holiday – droughts, **6** politics – rope

2 1 play, **2** send, **3** fridge, **4** alarm clock, **5** rainy, **6** vet, **7** pain

3 1 b, **2** b, **3** a, **4** c, **5** c, **6** a

4 1 has won/wins, **2** didn't/did not do, **3** will be, **4** getting up, **5** found, **6** 're/are watching

5 1 much, **2** –, **3** were, **4** better, **5** on, **6** Are

6 1 It's not your pen, it's mine! **2** My grandfather walks very slowly. **3** Don't go to the party if you don't like dancing. **4** There are ten girls in my class. **5** Sandra's very happy because she doesn't have to wear school uniform.

7 1 ✗, **2** ✗, **3** ✔, **4** ✔, **5** ✗, **6** ✗, **7** ✗, **8** ✔, **9** ✔, **10** ✗

8 1 d, **2** e, **3** b, **4** a, **5** c

9 1 healthier, **2** small, **3** phones, **4** often, **5** birthday

10 1 tickets/return, **2** qualities/have, **3** go/get, By, **4** come/idea, **5** language(s)/in

Elementary ↔ Pre-intermediate placement test

1 c, 2 d, 3 b, 4 d, 5 b, 6 a, 7 c, 8 b, 9 d, 10 b, 11 a, 12 d, 13 c, 14 a, 15 b, 16 c, 17 d, 18 a, 19 b, 20 b, 21 d, 22 b, 23 a, 24 c, 25 b, 26 c, 27 b, 28 a, 29 d, 30 c, 31 b, 32 a, 33 d, 34 c, 35 b, 36 b, 37 d, 38 b, 39 d, 40 b, 41 c, 42 d, 43 b, 44 b, 45 c, 46 a, 47 c, 48 b, 49 c, 50 a, 51 c, 52 c, 53 c, 54 b, 55 d, 56 c, 57 c, 58 d, 59 a, 60 b, 61 c, 62 d, 63 d, 64 a, 65 d, 66 d, 67 a, 68 b, 69 c, 70 b, 71 c, 72 a, 73 c, 74 b, 75 d, 76 c, 77 b, 78 c, 79 a, 80 b, 81 c, 82 d, 83 c, 84 d, 85 b, 86 c, 87 b, 88 a, 89 b, 90 c, 91 b, 92 c, 93 d, 94 d, 95 c, 96 a, 97 c, 98 b, 99 b, 100 c